S0-AAM-853

HUNTING HARD
FOR WHITETAILS

BILL WINKE

NORTH AMERICAN HUNTING CLUB

Minneapolis, Minnesota

COMPLETE DEER HUNTING LIBRARY

NORTH AMERICAN HUNTING CLUB

Mike Vail	Vice President, Products and Business Development
Tom Carpenter	Director of Book and New Media Development
Dan Kennedy	Book Production Manager
Michele Teigen	Book Development Coordinator

This book was originally published by Derrydale Press, Inc.

ISBN 0-914697-98-6

Printed in the United States of America
This book was printed on acid-free paper with 10 percent post-consumer recycled content.

NORTH★AMERICAN★HUNTING★CLUB

TABLE OF CONTENTS

EDITOR'S FOREWORD

Growing up, I could never figure out why my parents worked so hard even at home. They both had full-time jobs in town, but when they came home to our small farm in the evening and on weekends, they sure didn't relax. There were constant projects like gardening, barn painting, fence mending and lawn care.

Through the perspective of some years and some miles, I've gained an understanding of my parents' motives. Drives by the old place when I'm in that neck of the woods reveal that the farm has changed a lot! It's certainly no longer the envy of the neighborhood or a spot the tourists stopped to take pictures of.

My parents lived by the motto, "If you're going to do something, do it right!" In my adult life, I've adopted that philosophy in my home care, in my office work ... and in my hunting!

Doing it right, making the maximum commitment to trophy hunting is what Hunting Hard For Whitetails is all about! Some of the advice here may seem fanatical, but if you're really committed to hunting big white-tailed bucks then this blueprint honestly shows you what it takes to get the job done.

All of deer hunting does not take place in the woods, especially when you're talking about finding trophy bucks. To be consistently successful in this pursuit, you must make a commitment of lifestyle. That means hours of time devoted to poring over maps and record books, hours of contacting landowners and local hunters, hours of preparing yourself physically for the rigors of the hunt and mentally for waiting, long, cold hours alone in a stand only to be defeated again. Those are all hours you won't spend in "quality time" with the family or friends. Those are all hours you won't be earning a living or watching your favorite sports team.

Finally, you've got to be willing to expect and accept all the failures which will precede every success. Trophy bucks will make you look silly a lot more often than you'll make yourself look smart.

If you are willing to accept all of this, it means you're willing to do trophy whitetail hunting the right way, and this book will be an important guide. Enjoy this book. Hunt hard. Do it right.

Sincerely,

Bill

Bill Miller
Executive Director

CHAPTER ONE

WHAT IS SUCCESSFUL TROPHY HUNTING?

Hunting a seasoned old buck requires nearly as much mental homework as programming a computer or playing the stock market. You can't just flip a coin between IBM and Joe's Computer, nor should you pick your stand sites out of a hat. Each season—each day, for that matter—brings new options. To win this game, you should be trying to find the magical combination that allows you to go after a buck hard enough to have a chance of taking him, but not so hard that he knows he's being hunted. That, in a nutshell, is what hunting big whitetails is all about.

Many of the chapters in this book have to do with strategy—the mental side of deer hunting. I consider that the hard part. If you are going to gain some consistency at taking big whitetails you must first realize that your approach to the challenge—your mental approach—has more to do with success than how many ridges you can climb or how many stands you can put up in a day. It's fun to pull from what you know about whitetail behavior and then try to figure out ways to use it against them. It's like a chess game played over a huge, ever-changing playing field. You try to exploit any small weakness you can find.

Your alarm will become the trumpet blast that signals the day's events. You'll see some big bucks, and those visions will urge you on like a carrot on a string. And each evening you'll come dragging home, pull out your maps and try to figure out what went wrong. You'll drop unconscious into bed, looking forward to doing it all over again the next day. And after you've put in enough time, you'll know the sweet exhilaration that is yours when everything comes together, and a truly big buck steps into one of your shooting lanes.

Nothing approaches the thrill of a close encounter with a big buck. Adrenaline surges the instant you see the huge rack. It bobs easily from side-to-side, almost as if it is floating. Thick-necked and bull-chested, the buck shuffles steadily through the crunching leaves. Steam rises from his flaring nostrils on that crisp and frosty morning. Nose down, he makes his way straight toward you. With the moment of truth fast approaching, the excitement is almost more than you can bear. What is a front row seat at this drama worth? You'll know, because you've already paid for it. Regardless of the outcome of the moment, your time and effort have just been rewarded, with interest. That's the wonder of trophy whitetails.

CHAPTER TWO

FORMING A STRATEGY

I remember the first year that I seriously tried to hunt only big, trophy bucks. I was living in southern Michigan at the time, and had received permission from my barber to hunt on his family farm. I didn't realize at the time what I had, but the family's 1,000-acre property was almost exclusively mine.

My game plan was simple: find the spot with the most sign and put up a stand. I didn't give any thought to travel corridors, or how my presence in the area around those stands would impact deer behavior. I didn't even try to consider where they were bedding or feeding as I focused entirely upon buck sign. Without a real plan, my approach was as fickle as the Indian summer breezes that filtered through the property's hardwoods.

If, on the first day, I didn't see the buck that had left all the sign, I figured I was in the wrong spot. My confidence and patience would flag, and off I'd go in search of a "better" stand. If I saw a nice buck in the distance I'd head right over there as soon as I could, and put up a stand. I was always one step behind the action. I made enough mistakes that year to last a lifetime, and ended the season without one of the dandy bucks that roamed the property.

What I learned from that season of frustration is the motivation for this chapter. I found that you need to stay one step ahead of the action if you want to take a trophy buck, and to do that you need a well-thought-out game plan, and enough faith to see it through. If you begin changing your basic strategy every time things don't work out, the chances for consistent success on trophy bucks are unlikely, at best.

I've chosen to use this chapter as a building block for the rest of the book. I'll develop only a few basic principles here that have become my doctrine of big buck hunting. Despite the fact that there are many different ways to tag a trophy, there are only a few concrete and incontrovertible facts about whitetails, and how to hunt them, that can't be compromised. As long as you live by these fundamentals you can do pretty much anything that makes sense at the time. Really understanding these few key points is where the whole process of trophy hunting begins.

DON'T LET HIM KNOW HE'S BEING HUNTED

Maybe the single most important element of big buck strategy is the element of surprise. It can't be overstated. If a big buck knows he's being hunted, whether by you or someone else, your chances of tagging him in that general area are slim. The element of surprise is that important. Everything you do from the time you enter the woods until the time you leave it should be a calculated and deliberate balancing act. On one side of the pivot you have the desire to push things hard enough to get within range of a big buck. And on the other side is the desire to keep a low profile so that if you aren't successful in tagging the big one today there will still be a tomorrow.

Once a smart old buck runs across your scent on the ground, or sees you walking to your stand, or even sees or smells you while you're actually on stand, his behavior

Most hunters head straight for the areas with the best buck sign. Often, this is not the best approach.

changes. First, he'll become highly suspicious and careful in his home range, making him very difficult to see during the daylight. He'll most certainly change his movement patterns. Finally, if your presence continues for a couple of days he may actually move out of the area completely–or become entirely nocturnal–as he realizes his "safe area" isn't safe anymore.

Let me put a big buck's reaction to our presence into human terms: Suppose you got up in the morning and found someone's Ronald McDonald Happy Meal box and an empty oil jug laying along the street in front of your home. You would know someone had been past there, but you wouldn't think a whole lot of it, would you? Now suppose you found those same items in your living room! No doubt there would be some security changes around your home. It is the same with mature whitetails.

When a big buck realizes someone has invaded his living room, he takes security measures. So the trick is to sneak in and out of their living rooms without them knowing it (a difficult task, to say the least). Or, we can wait for them in stands located outside of these sensitive areas—in places where the evidence of our passing won't be taken as seriously. Now there's something to think about.

Much of trophy hunting is a science, especially when you get down to deer behavior, but the ability to balance pursuit with stealth is a real art. That part of the hunt is something that can't be spelled out in recip-ebook fashion. There are no absolutes, as each situation is different. How to apply this delicate balance will form much of the basis for the following chapters in this book.

FOCUS ON INCREASING YOUR ODDS

On the surface, the concept of odds seems a little too obvious to be an important key to success, but like an iceberg floating harmlessly in the north Atlantic, there is more here than you first perceive. Attention to detail is an important part of any endeavor, and no less so when the quest is trophy deer. Each step of the hunt—each little thing you consider doing or not doing—should be evaluated. How does it affect your odds? Even if the improvement in your chances is only slight, it is worth the effort. Enough small things eventually add up to big things, and a couple of percentage points added here, and a few there, may be all that is required to put you into the biggest buck of your life.

A simple example might help. It was a special muzzle-loader hunt during the 1995 season on a waterfowl refuge in Illinois. They didn't allow any advance scouting, and I had never set foot on the place before that morning. So here I was in the pitch dark without a map, trying to come

The author took this nice buck during the 1995 season. He set up in a spot where many trails intersected, dramatically increasing his odds.

up with a game plan! I got back into the woods a little ways and began slowly still-hunting until I found what I was looking for.

The funnel was formed by a large pond and a water-filled moat. About 100 yards of mostly open cover separated the two. At least eight different trails came close enough together there to be covered from a single position. A few dozen does made their way through early, but the first two hours were pretty dead. Finally the rest of the hunters on the refuge began to mill around. In the next half hour I saw roughly 150 deer come through that funnel! I shot the biggest buck I saw, a well framed 10-pointer with a broken tine. I had stumbled onto a spot that drove my odds sky-high.

Chapter Three is devoted to many more steps you can take to improve your odds. If you get good enough at this you'll eventually raise them to the point where your chances for success each season are actually good!

MASTER THE WIND

I remember my introduction to the mysterious world of swirling breezes. I was hunting a deep ravine in river break country bordering the upper Mississippi River. The wind was from the perfect direction to blow my scent directly away from the big scrape I was watching–or so I thought. With great anticipation, I slipped into my big-buck hotspot only to find that down in the bottom of the ravine, the wind was actually reversed, blowing in the opposite direction!

Every time the wind gusted, my scent was spread all over that draw, up and down. Finally, at the end of the day I slunk out of there, thoroughly disgusted with myself.

Never stop learning about white-tailed deer. Whenever you encounter sign, or observe a certain kind of behavior, ask yourself why the deer did what it did. An inquisitive mind will make you a better hunter.

Every deer in the ravine had smelled me and taken off in a snorting, stamping frenzy. In a single session on stand I had ruined what I felt was my best spot.

I think you'll be surprised at how much better your hunting strategy becomes with a thorough understanding of the wind. You'll be able to predict the type of swirling zephyrs that once ruined your hunts. You'll know how to make the lay of the land, and changes in cover density, work for you. I firmly believe that once you learn to master the wind, success is inevitable–becoming just a matter of putting in enough time on stand. Scooping the wind will be the subject of Chapter Nine.

UNDERSTANDING DEER BEHAVIOR

Many times you'll sit back and ask yourself "What do I do next?" The answer to that question lies in your understanding of what the bucks are likely to do next. The more you know about deer behavior under many different conditions and at every phase of the season, the better will be the choices that you make while hunting.

Study everything you can find that offers proven information on deer behavior. While scientific data is great, little is available relative to trophy-class bucks. For years, hunting writers have been offering theories about big bucks, and why they do what they do. Though not based on scientific studies, some of this information is still very helpful in shedding new light, especially when it comes from people who are actually tagging big bucks!

There's not enough room for me to get deeply into the subject of deer behavior here. Instead, I'll be focusing almost strictly on strategy, but some thoughts on behavior are woven into these pages, nonetheless. Go beyond this book, and even beyond the Complete Deer Hunting Library, and absorb as much information as possible. Spend time in the woods studying deer sign and asking yourself "why?" Learn all you can because knowledge is one of the primary keys to successful trophy hunting.

CHAPTER THREE

INCREASING YOUR ODDS

You have to base your decisions on something. I like to base mine on how my odds for success are affected. Some steps that you take can have a huge impact on your odds. Don't overlook a single one of them.

LOCATION AFFECTS YOUR ODDS

In trophy hunting, as in real estate, location is everything. Before you can pick the right tree, you have to pick the right property. And in some cases, the quest may even take you to a different state or county. This is the hunt before the hunt, and it is the most difficult part of trophy hunting. No amount of stealth and woodsmanship will make up for an area devoid of big bucks. Most consistently successful trophy hunters are good woodsmen, but I'll guarantee you that all of them hunt the very best places they can find.

Finding the best hunting areas is hard, time-consuming work. You need to talk to a lot of people and walk a lot of ground before you know the absolute best spots to hunt each season. Good farms and bad farms are often found within a mile of each other. And things change from year to year depending upon crop rotation, as well as the success rates and hunting practices of the local gun hunters.

If there are three good bucks on a 300-acre farm, your

odds of tagging one are roughly three times better than on a similarly sized farm where there is only one. It's that simple. Once you've identified a hotspot, do what you have to do (short of trespassing, of course) to get on there.

I've put up tens of thousands of hay bales, and planted fence posts until my hands bled, just to gain and keep hunting rights. As a result, I've made some great friends, and I've never lost access to a single good piece of ground once I've gained it. These days I hunt the absolute best places I can find in several different states. I'll never apologize for that, and neither should you. There are a lot of sacrifices involved in getting there. Regardless of what you may think, excellent hunting areas are still available for those willing to look hard.

STAND PLACEMENT AFFECTS YOUR ODDS

Several springs ago I found a good rubline along the side of a ridge while scouting. That fall I grabbed a portable stand and went back. The rubline had been reworked, and without considering my options further, I simply put up the stand and began waiting. Before the day was over a really nice 10-pointer had given me the slip.

I knew even as I was putting the stand up that I was violating my number one rule in stand placement, but I was too lazy that day to exert the teaspoon of extra effort it would have taken to get that buck. This rule is simple: never put up a stand to cover only one travel route when you can cover two. Never cover only two when you can cover three, etc. Day-in and day-out, it is a simple rule that makes a big difference.

I should have slipped along the rubline until I came to a position that would have allowed me to also cover the

Having an open shot to any deer that approaches within range is an important way to increase your odds. You'd be surprised how many hunters don't consider this.

Every minute you sit on stand brings you one minute closer to getting a shot at a nice buck. That mindset will keep you out there hunting when others are napping in front of the TV.

ridge-top trail without giving my wind away. It wouldn't have been a tough stunt because I knew the ridge-top trail would be there. The big buck slipped past just out of range two hours after I set up the stand.

That buck reinforced a central theme in trophy strategy: Never quit looking for ways to improve your odds. It seems that painful lessons are the best teachers.

Here's one that's even more painful. During a season several years ago, I helped my buddy Mike Sawyer pick out a spot for his treestand. We wanted to get in and out quickly, without leaving a lot of scent, so as a result we didn't check things out as well as we should have. We picked what seemed like a good spot. From that stand Mike saw several impressive bucks, each just out of range. The clincher came near the end of the rut, however.

A rack the likes of which he'll never see again came bobbing up the fence line–heading directly toward Mike. According to my friend, the 12-point typical had at least a two-foot inside spread, great mass, and better than foot-long tines. The mighty buck was a legend maker. Instead of continuing along the fence, right past Mike's drawn bow, he stopped 60 yards away. The buck looked around for a few moments before jumping the fence. Mike allows that he will never forget the sight of those huge antlers floating easily over the barbed wire and disappearing forever in the weed field beyond.

That world-class buck taught us two tough lessons. Mike was covering a fence line which comprised only one travel route. (Remember my number one rule of stand placement?) We should've looked up and down the fence until we came to the perpendicular trail the buck had used. In hindsight, it was an obvious thing to see. The trail was there as big as day. Mike still would have been covering the fence line, and would have had a possible world-record right in his lap.

The second lesson is just as important. If you are going to put up a stand that you will be using several times during the season, make sure you get the job done right the first time. What you gain by leaving the few extra tracks required to find a high-odds stand location far outweighs the negative affects of a little additional human scent left behind.

What if there was one tree on each of the pieces of property you hunt that every big buck eventually has to walk past? Trying to find it will change the way you think about your hunting area. What you'll find are better stand sites than any you've sat in before–spots where your odds will really skyrocket. The trick is knowing what constitutes a big buck travel route, but we'll get to that in later chapters. First we need to look at some more ways to up your odds.

SHOOTING LANES AFFECT YOUR ODDS

Rod Ponton lives to bowhunt big whitetails in his home state of Kansas. Rod has hunted several truly giant whitetails in the past decade, but none can compare to the one he almost took in 1990. Rod saw a tremendous typical from a treestand in 1989, and slipped along the ground to within 60 yards of the buck. He was awesome! A 10-pointer with incredible mass, width, and tine length. No stranger to big bucks, Rod is sure the G-4s (fourth point on each beam) were still well over 12 inches in length! There's no telling what that buck would've scored, but the fact that he was framed up as a potential world-record contender cannot be denied.

Anything you can do to reduce the distance a deer can smell you will improve your odds. This hunter his outerwear clean, wears activated charcoal clothing and even keeps his rubber boots in a scent-proof container.

The more big bucks in the areas you hunt, the higher your odds will be. Spend lots of time actually looking for outsized bucks.

During 1990, Rod hunted that buck, and only that buck. "He was following a doe when I saw him again in the middle of November that second year," said Ponton. "They were both coming down a trail, and they were breathing hard like they had been doing a lot of chasing. The doe stopped short and the buck goosed her. She trotted right past the hedge tree I was sitting in, perfectly through my shooting lane. Instead of following her, he went on the other side of the tree, away from the trail. I didn't have a shooting lane in that direction so all I could do was watch. He was only about 12 yards away. I could have spit on him, but I had no shot. I never saw him again after that."

What would my friend have given for an opening to shoot through on the opposite side of the twisted hedge tree? The simple decision of whether or not to open another shooting lane can have more to do with tagging a trophy than how well you handle your gun or bow.

Several seasons ago I climbed into an afternoon stand.

In placing your stand: "Don't give anything away"

While stand A was not in a bad spot, stand B would have been a much better location. Not only could the bowhunter cover any deer following the fenceline, but also any deer using the heavy fence crossing. When placing a stand (especially one that will be used several times) always find the absolute best spot. Cover as many travel options as you can.

Going over all the possible shot opportunities and how I would handle each one, I kept coming back to one area in front of me where I had no possible shot. After sitting in the stand for over an hour I couldn't take it any longer. I climbed down and cleared two wrist-thick saplings and a couple of low limbs. I was quickly back up in the tree. Within an hour a great buck stopped momentarily right in that opening. I got him, but had I not trimmed out the lane shortly before, I wouldn't even have gotten a shot.

I'll get into more detail on shooting lanes, and where to put them, in the next chapter, which deals specifically with treestand placement and preparation. Here, it is enough to say that your ability to cover the area around your stand has a tremendous affect on your odds for success. Though they may try, no one can tell you which side of the tree a trophy buck will walk on. Forget about where the trails are located. Every "dead zone" around your stand reduces your odds for success.

LITTLE THINGS AFFECT YOUR ODDS

The list of hunters whose dreams have been shattered by small equipment malfunctions is long and particularly bitter. I know a guy who had a *bonafide* Boone & Crockett buck at 15 yards. His treestand squeaked as he shifted his weight while drawing his bow. The buck bolted. I saw it on video. Another of my friends had a similarly painful experience. Another giant B & C trophy was coming in to rattling when the hunter's stand cracked as he shifted his weight that cold, still morning. At 60 yards the buck turned tail. Paying attention to every aspect of your equipment and not taking anything for granted will increase your odds for success.

Small things can ruin your hunt. Take care of every detail, including making sure your treestands don't squeak when you shift your weight. Be sure to use scent-free oil.

Can you increase your odds by shortening the range at which a deer can scent you? You bet you can! Is it worth the extra effort? You tell me. That is what playing the odds comes down to: these types of decisions. Hunters who are willing to put out the effort to address every detail of the hunt are the ones who seem to be "lucky" enough to bag big bucks on a regular basis.

AMOUNT OF TIME ON STAND AFFECTS YOUR ODDS

When I'm sitting on stand I can mentally picture the meter slowly turning. In the morning it might read 75 percent. At noon maybe its 76 percent. By the time I climb down it's 78 percent. Eventually it's going to reach 100 percent and my time will come to draw my bow on another big one. The better you do with the other factors in this chapter, the faster the meter turns, but it will happen eventually. It has to. Time on stand is the practical part of hunting strategy. It is where the rubber meets the road. Without time on stand everything else in this chapter is worthless philosophy. Each minute you hunt takes you one minute closer to tagging the buck of your dreams.

There is more to persistence than just hunting every day. You have to do your best to be in each stand when it is most likely to produce action. You can accomplish this by having plenty of stands to choose from and then spot-checking them occasionally to find out which ones are the hottest. By slipping carefully in and checking the sign in the general area of each stand you can tell when the deer are really using the location. I look for large tracks much the same way a bear guide studies the ground to identify his best baits for producing bulky bruins. By looking first in fringe areas, such as road crossings and field edges, you don't run the risk of messing up a sensitive hunting area before you even get a chance to hunt it.

Hunting all day is a sure way to increase your stand time, and your odds, but it can be an incredible battle with boredom. I can only do it for a few days in a row, so I only hammer it during the peak of the rut. Bucks will move all day at these times, and success can come at any moment. Since I don't work for a living–that's what my wife says anyway–I get to hunt more than almost anyone I know. But even people with real jobs can increase their stand time by taking advantage of those precious minutes before and after work each day. Every minute is important. Don't ever forget that.

I used a lot of screw-ups to illustrate my points in this chapter. It is easier to learn valuable lessons from painful experiences than from pleasant ones. Every time a big buck gets away, there's usually a lesson to be learned. I've had more than my share of these sessions, and each time the answer came down to laziness in one of the areas discussed in this chapter. Remember, everything you do, or don't do, will affect your odds for success.

CHAPTER FOUR

STAND PLACEMENT AND PREPARATION

At a recent outdoor trade show, a couple of western big-game hunters cornered me and proceeded to "educate" me on the real truth about hunting. Apparently, my favorite form of hunting is boring. That's what I was told, anyway. "Where's the hunting?" they mocked. "All you're doing is sitting around."

I explained to my dubious friends that the "hunting" in stand hunting takes place over a period of weeks, even months, before the day when the trigger is actually pulled or the string released. Choosing a place to put your stand is more like a chess game than random selection.

With one small adjustment in your stand location, the outcome of your entire season, possibly your whole hunting career, can change. Just like in chess, you have to foresee the possible outcomes and make your moves accordingly. The following hunt, which took place a couple seasons back, is a good illustration of the process.

I was hunting a portion of creek bottom in one of the plains states. From a stand set up mostly for observation, I saw deer crossing an alfalfa field as they headed toward their bedding area on a brushy bend in the creek. At noon that day I slipped in and carefully chose a place for my treestand. Instead of making things easy by coming out of the woods in only one location, the deer were using three or four trails, spread over a distance of nearly 50 yards. In addition, a nice trail ran down through the bottom of the adjacent draw which bordered the field here.

Not wanting to give up a single travel route, I spent a full hour standing in one place deciding which tree allowed me to cover everything. I was hunting with a bow, making the task of covering everything more difficult. By giving up even one trail, I would be reducing my chances of taking a good buck by as much as 20 to 25 percent. Finally, I made my decision and picked a tree which was downwind of two out of three trails, while still within range of the one along the bottom of the draw. This left one trail on my downwind side. In order to eliminate the risk of being winded by deer passing along this last trail, I knew I would have to put the stand relatively high, between 18 and 20 feet up, so that my scent would drift over their heads.

With the mental work done, the physical work began. I had to put the stand up and carefully open discrete shooting lanes to each of the several travel routes. Bear in mind that I was planning on hunting the stand the very next morning. Such a quick turn-around wouldn't allow deer to get used to any significant changes I might make, nor for my scent to be erased.

So I had to be extra careful. Once the stand was up, I scrutinized what I had, going over in my mind how I would attempt every possible shot, should it arise. If a reasonable opening already existed I would move on to the next trail, otherwise I would note the minimum number of branches that had to be removed for open shooting.

Climbing down, I went straight to each area and quickly did my trimming, taking great pains to keep from leaving too much scent. Now I was ready. Anything that came within 30 yards of my stand from any direction would be forced to offer at least one good shot. I had taken the time

This big eight-pointer fell to the author's arrow in mid-November of 1994. The buck was the result of careful stand placement.

No matter how good the location, a stand is not a great stand unless you can approach it without bumping into deer or allowing them to catch your scent.

to increase my odds as high as possible. The real hunting was completed, now it was just a waiting game.

I had been on stand for nearly three hours the following morning when the guttural grunt of a buck electrified the cool November air. Thirty seconds later he materialized, following two does and two fawns across the narrow brushy draw. As I readied myself, all five deer came up one of the trails that led toward the hay field. At a range of 25 yards, my arrow took the heavy-bodied, massive-horned eight-pointer behind the front leg just as he stepped into the narrow shooting lane I had opened the day before.

Those deer had used a faint trail, the one I had least expected to produce action. Leaving nothing to chance, I had prepared a shot in that direction anyway. I'm very glad I did! It is critical that you be able to get a good shot at any deer that passes within range of your stand.

ADJUST YOUR STRATEGY TO CHANGING DEER BEHAVIOR

In Chapter Two, I stressed the importance of staying one step ahead of the action. Let's take a simplified look at buck behavior, and ways to exploit it, during each part of the season.

In the early and late seasons, most of what you do should be geared around what you have seen. Since the mature buck's primary focus is on feeding at these times, you must find him at his feeding area first and work backward. You can use fresh sign (especially really big tracks) to help, but finding him in the first place will always be the toughest part. The only real trick is remaining undetected as does pass your stand. Spook the does and you'll never see the bucks that so often lag behind. In fact, if you spook a buck on a feeding pattern, you may never see him again for the rest of the season.

The biggest buck I've ever had close got away because of just such an event. The perfect 10-pointer (for those who care, I'm guessing he'd push 180 B & C) came out and passed just out of bow range. Not worrying, I figured I'd get another chance the next evening, but when a doe got downwind of me and began snorting and stamping, he evaporated in a stiff-legged walk. Though I hunted the field carefully for the next two weeks, I never saw him again. When hunting feeding patterns, it is best to hang back until you have things well figured out. Many times you'll only get one crack, so make it a good one.

Patterns are fine early and late in the season, but during the peak of the rut it is rare that you'll spot an individual buck doing the same thing more than once. By relying upon tendencies instead of actual sightings, you can set up stands for bucks you've never seen. Since they're moving a lot early in the rut, travel routes are very effective places to sit and wait. Rather than try to work out the patterns of an individual buck at this time, you'll be much less frustrated if you hunt a specific class of bucks and take the first one that fills the bill.

Here are a couple of tips for stand placement during the rut. First, before the does begin to come into estrus, look for bucks traveling between two bedding areas. Any funnel that connects two large areas of cover will do. Picking the right tree can be tricky since these routes are rarely used at other times of the season and the amount of buck sign there will be very limited. Look for anything that will concentrate movement and trust your judgment.

Later, as the does begin to come into estrus and breeding begins in earnest, start "hunting" does. Big

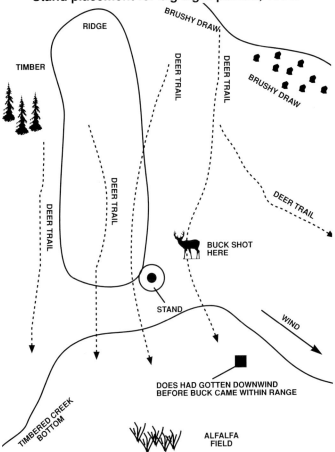

Stand placement strategies
Stand placement for big eight-pointer, 1994.

The stand site was chosen so that all trails would be within range. Any deer heading toward the field would have to offer a shot. Only one trail was downwind and that is the one he used, but the stand was high enough that the does didn't scent the author. Small shooting lanes were opened to every trail. The buck was actually shot on the trail the author felt least likely to produce action, proving you can never take anything for granted in this game.

bucks can still be found in the same places you found them in the pre-breeding phase, but now you will also find many of them actually following does. That means trails used by does to get from their bedding to feeding areas become buck magnets, and placing stands where several come together is an excellent strategy. You'll notice by all the scrapes you find that bucks know where these spots are too.

PICKING THE RIGHT TREE

All else being equal, the stand that is within range of the most travel routes is the best one. But trails aren't the only travel routes used by bucks. Learn to recognize everything that influences buck movement.

Big bucks try to use the terrain to keep a low profile when moving, and will go out of their way to remain unseen. These travel routes will not be used often, nor will there be a lot of buck sign. Oftentimes you simply have to fly by faith, and wait to see the results. If all of your hunting in the past has been over obvious sign, this will be a tough step for you. But once you take it, you'll find yourself hunting a different class of buck. I'll get into greater detail on how to read the terrain for travel routes in Chapter Eight.

Funnels are excellent places to locate stands whether you're hunting with a bow or a gun—even when hunting from the ground. As mentioned, terrain can funnel deer. Available cover also funnels deer. Since mature bucks prefer to remain hidden when traveling, they will take advantage of any cover between point A and point B. Funnels can be very subtle, such as small breaks in the terrain or sidehill benches. They can also be more obvious, such as

The new generation of affordable laser rangefinders are a tremendous benefit to bowhunters, allowing them to establish very accurate range references without leaving human scent all over the hunting area.

fence lines, and necks of dry land near rivers, ponds, lakes or swamps. The list of funnels is endless. You'll find plenty of them where you hunt if you'll just start looking.

Broad funnels, such as a wide bench or draw, pose a problem because it is often impossible to cover the entire corridor from a stand put up along its downwind edge. We've all been told that you have to stay downwind of deer at all costs. But, sometimes it makes more sense to be up-wind of them! A stand 18 to 20 feet off the ground (or higher) will permit a steady breeze to carry your scent above a deer's nose for approximately 20 yards, under good conditions. That buys you 20 more yards of coverage. Bowhunters should immediately see the value of this.

Deer can smell a person up to a half-mile away. That means that whenever you walk to your stand with a cross-wind blowing at your side, you are telling every deer in a huge area that you've arrived. Rather than first putting up a stand in a great spot and then compromising it later when you approach to hunt it, you are much better off working backwards.

A stand is not a great stand if it can't be approached without spooking deer. One spot I hunted during a recent season is a perfect example. The location itself was excellent. Huge tracks from more than one big buck littered the picked cornfield on the ridge-top, indicating that at least one bomber buck was using the area heavily. In the bordering woods, I found a narrow funnel between the top of a steep ditch and the field edge that forced all the deer to pass through an area only 40 yards wide. With the prevailing winds, I could set up with my scent blowing out toward the open field and never have to worry about being scented. It was the kind of spot that I literally spend weeks looking for.

Early and late in the season, when big bucks are somewhat pattern-able, it is critical that you hang back from activity areas until you have a good idea what is taking place there. You may only get one good crack once you move in.

There was only one weak link in what should have been a chain of events leading to the tagging of a big buck. I knew it would be tough to get to the stand in the morning because deer feeding in the open field would spook at my passing. I couldn't drop down into the woods and come to the stand from the valley below because it was all private property and permission there had already been denied. I elected to wait until just before sunrise, well after first light, to sneak in. I reasoned that by such time all the deer would be in the woods, and I could beat them to my stand as they headed to bed on the brushy point beyond it.

The first morning I hunted the spot I was zipping along at a fast clip when I heard a deer snort down to my right, along the edge of the woods. Several does followed by a dandy 10-pointer, probably scoring 150+, ran along the edge and then jumped the fence into the woods.

I was sick. I sat in my stand all day, but the only buck to come along was a little six-pointer.

I had blown it. Morning access to that stand was poor. It was a great stand, but not in the morning. I never should have been there.

In small cover situations where you have to cross open ground to get to the trees, your approach may well be the most important aspect of the hunt. Go well out of your way to take advantage of low spots in fields and bands of cover such as shelter belts and fence lines. The last thing you want to do is skyline yourself, even in the dark.

It is a lot of work to go to such extremes when simply getting to your stand, but that is the price you must sometimes pay to keep that big bruiser from knowing you are hunting him. Now I never put up a stand unless I know I can get to and from it without taking any chances of being seen or scented. Instead of just an afterthought, undetected access should become your number-one stand-placement criteria.

PREPPING THE TREE

Once you've chosen the perfect tree, you need to set it up correctly. All you're trying to do is guarantee yourself at least one good shot at anything within range, regardless of where it shows up. Forget about trails now, bucks don't always follow them. Just clear lanes, however small, in every direction.

If you are putting a stand up shortly after the season, and won't be hunting it for months, you can get away with a lot of pruning and disturbance. Even at that, keep it down so as not to remove all the silhouette-breaking cover. On the other hand, if you will be hunting the stand in the near future, don't disturb things any more than you have to. A missing limb here or there isn't noticed by a buck on the move, but a wholesale clearcut will be immediately evident. And the scent you leave while playing lumberjack is just as detrimental.

An important step when setting up a stand, especially if you're a bowhunter, is getting range references. I keep a small spiral note pad in my fanny pack that I use to jot down the distance from each stand to many reference points around it. The new, price-conscious laser rangefinders, such as Bushnell's Lytespeed, are an excellent investment for the bowhunter, and can be used quickly to scope out many reference points each time you go on stand. Some hunters like to put out color-coded range markers. This may be all right if you won't be hunting the stand for a long time. Otherwise, it's not a good idea to leave human scent all over for passing deer to deal with.

Rehearsal is your final step in preparing for the moment of truth. Every time you get into your stand, familiarize yourself with the openings that you have designated as shooting lanes.

In your mind's eye, visualize that big buck coming from every possible direction, and at every possible distance, within your maximum shooting range. How will you handle each encounter?

That knowledge is incredibly valuable, and gaining it before the buck actually shows up is the key to reacting decisively.

Recently, I had a very nice buck approach a stand from a direction that I had not been prepared for. He showed up quickly, cresting a small hill right in front of me. He paused for a moment and then took off at a fast walk. In a panic, I quickly tried to pick an opening in front of him for the shot. My arrow deflected off a branch right before it got to the buck. I had blown it. I am continually reminded that you can't take anything for granted in this sport.

CHAPTER FIVE

MINIMUM-IMPACT TROPHY HUNTING

The farmer's soft, easy words rocked me like a hard right hook to the jaw. "I just walked into the woods and sat down and there he was," said Charlie. My friend had decided to do a little fall turkey hunting, one of his favorite pastimes. He had gone up on the knob, on a part of his farm near a stand where I'd spent many fruitless hours. He proceeded to pick a stump and pull out his call.

"Well, a little before sunset I saw this smaller buck come out of the cornfield a short distance away. He was following a doe. A few minutes later I got ready to leave. I just happened to look over my shoulder and there stood the most beautiful buck you can imagine. His rack was tall and wide. I suppose if I'd had a bow I could have shot him right there."

"Yeah, I saw him up there from the road through binoculars a couple of days ago," I replied. "He was massive, with a long drop tine off his left beam." Then, from my lofty perch of false assurance, I elaborated on the size of the drop-tine buck, how his typical frame would have scored in the 150s or 160s, and how I had tried to sneak in front of him, but to no avail.

Charlie smiled politely. "Yeah, I know which one you're talking about," he said. "That drop-tine buck was the smaller one that was followin' the doe. The other one was *huge*."

WHAM! My eyes rolled back and my knees started

to buckle from the impact of the vicious blow. A few moments of silence and then I heard a loud pop. It was my bubble bursting.

I looked down at my boot toe as I kicked weakly at the big tire on Charlie's combine. I could only shake my head in bewilderment. How many times had I heard this story? It seemed the two weeks I had just spent busting my hump had been a total waste of time. All I had to do was "just walk into the woods and pick a stump."

Think back on all the stories you've heard from squirrel hunters, turkey hunters, beginners, etc. involving a close encounter with a truly huge buck. The odds seem staggering against such an occurrence, yet it happens with agonizing regularity. I remember the guy that "accidentally" wandered into one of my best hunting areas in the pre-dawn darkness. With no more knowledge of the area than the fact that he had found a climbable tree, he erected his stand in time to watch 31 deer pass in the course of a couple of hours. Three were P & Y class bucks, with one being the huge 10-pointer I'd hunted for the previous week without ever seeing him. Give me a break! Is this sport just pure luck?

What do all these occurrences have in common? What is there about "beginner's luck" that makes it such a good strategy for monster bucks? What could I learn from these seemingly accidental successes that could be applied to improve my chances for a really outstanding buck? That's the question I wrestled with as I drove the quarter mile down Charlie's driveway, and for days afterward.

What I took from that day has affected the way I've hunted trophy bucks every season since. I finally realized that beginners are the ultimate low-impact hunters. What could offer less warning than simply walking into the woods and choosing a spot that "just felt good?" No scouting. No scent left from a previous trip. Nothing to give an ultra-suspicious

Every time you scout your hunting area, put up a stand, or just walk to and from your stand you leave ground scent. When deer encounter it, they become harder to tag in that area.

The best time to scout is after the season. At that time you can comb your hunting area, choose spots for future stands and even put a few stands up that can be used in the mornings during the coming season.

buck notice that something is up. Before I tell you how I applied this knowledge, we first need to look at important factor in balancing our impact: human ground scent.

I was heading to a great stand, maybe my best that year. I had seen some dandy bucks from it in past seasons, and I was looking forward to a repeat performance. Fifteen yards from the stand I had to cross a well-used deer trail that lay between the withered yellow corn stalks I had just snuck through and the field's brushy perimeter. I decided to jump across the deer trail just to make sure that I wouldn't leave any scent within three feet of it.

The first group of does and fawns came past 45 minutes later. The lead doe hit my crossing and immediately locked up. What could she possibly be smelling? The wind was blowing straight from her to me, I had worn knee-high rubber boots, washed my clothes in unscented soap, showered before the hunt, sprayed scent eliminator on my pants legs, even danced a jig in a "cow pie" before entering the corn field.

Finally, without flagging, blowing, or otherwise signalling her alarm, the doe simply reversed course and slipped quietly into the standing corn, taking the rest of the herd with her. *Dang! what a spooky doe*, I thought to myself. *I haven't been in this area for a whole year!*

A half hour later another good sized group of does and fawns waltzed up the trail. (Where were all the bucks on this perfect November morning?) As I sat petrified in my tree, their carefree movements immediately changed to visible tension as the whole herd stumbled into the leader who again had frozen on point at my trail crossing. The performance of the first group was repeated, and these deer also faded into the corn.

The final blow came when a single yearling doe came walking up the trail with her head held high and simply turned inside out when she hit my entry trail. First, she dashed one direction, and then the other. She really wanted to cross my path but apparently feared for her very life should she do so. Finally, gathering all her speed and courage, she sprang high in the air, completely clearing the area containing my scent before racing madly into the nearby woods. That left me sick and empty, as if I had just witnessed a traffic accident. I knew I could never beat a deer's nose, no matter how hard I tried. Seeing how they reacted left little doubt that I was messing up my stands every time I hunted them. And so are you! It was the most depressing day I had ever spent in a treestand, but it was also the most enlightening. I obviously needed to give more thought to the subject of managing human ground scent.

As you leave the woods, your airborne scent leaves with you. Ground scent, on the other hand, remains for days in some cases, alerting every deer that runs across it, long after we go home.

I've had thousands of opportunities to watch deer react to ground scent. In certain parts of the country, especially in dry climes and in areas with high deer densities, they seem to pay it less mind. Young deer will let you get by with more, sniffing the ground and brush a few times before going on about their business. And there are areas where people are more common in the woods, causing deer to become somewhat desensitized. Yet even under the best of conditions, I've never seen a mature buck (or doe, for that matter) walk past my scent trail without getting nervous and taking some form of evasive action as a result. By now you should see that left-over human scent plays a major role in determining your trophy success rate.

Have you ever wondered why the first time you sit on a stand is usually the best time? Residual ground scent is one of the main reasons, especially if the stand is located right in an

The author took this nice 10-pointer in 1992. On this hunt he went into an area he had never been in before, using an aerial photo to choose the best stand area.

area with high deer activity. Each successive time you hunt the stand, you leave more scent and educate more deer (in a number of different ways) until the spot becomes deer hunting's version of a ghost town.

If you try to hunt an area more than once or twice, chances are that any resident mature buck is going to know he is being hunted long before you get a crack at him. The buck only needs to make one nocturnal trip across your trail to know that his previously safe, undisturbed haven of refuge is now being invaded by a human. In many cases he'll simply move on, or use the area only after he has carefully checked it out from downwind. Either way, you lose. Cruising bucks may still pass through the area, but once all of the mature does have wised up and changed their behavior, even cruisers are unlikely visitors.

There are other forms of human impact besides ground scent. They can see you in the stand, or walking to and from it, or if the wind swirls or shifts slightly deer will smell you. All of these events spell trouble, especially when they occur more than once.

Every discussion on the subject of human impact always finds its way back to a central issue: your best chance to take a trophy buck is the first time you venture into his domain. This being true, why not make every time on stand a first time? How is that possible? Let's go back to the story I started at the beginning of this chapter.

After leaving my friend Charlie's farm those many years ago, I became struck by the fact that I needed a different approach to trophy hunting. I needed a strategy that allowed me to take advantage of the strengths of the beginner. Then it occurred to me: I too would just walk into a spot I had not been to for months, or maybe never. I'd simply pick a spot that felt good, put up a stand and start hunting. I somehow knew it would work and two days later I found out.

Aerial photos are the key to low-impact treestand hunting. You can study the photos at home during your free time to pinpoint stand locations without ever having to leave scent in your hunting area.

I hadn't seen a thing that morning, even though it was dead calm and frosty, with the rut in full swing. By the time I left my stand I had already made up my mind that my afternoon hunt was going to be in a completely fresh area. As soon as I got home I pulled out my aerial photos, looking for a place I knew had deer but had not been hunted (or even scouted)

When hunting a new area for the first time, you will often be forced to choose more open trees so you will be assured of a good shot when a buck comes past.

that season. I found what I was looking for on a farm that I had been given permission to hunt only a month before.

From the photo, I could see a narrow draw that connected several fingers of brush and trees with a large block of timber. It seemed the perfect spot to ambush a cruising buck. As closely as possible, I picked an ambush from the photo. Shortly after noon I snuck directly to the spot with my stand on my back.

While standing in one place, I could see a spot where two good trails came together on my side (the downwind side) of the draw. I chose a tree that would allow me to cover both trails, as well as any random movement down through the bottom of the draw. It just felt good! Using tree steps, I quickly climbed the tree, then slipped the pin-mounted Vantage Point stand off my back and quietly into place. I climbed on, trimmed a couple of limbs and pulled up my bow. I was hunting.

Just before sunset a nice 10-pointer came into view. Cutting across the draw, he began following one of the trails right toward me. Head down, he was scent checking for does as he worked my way at a steady pace. Broadside, at a range of only 12 yards, I couldn't miss. In that one successful afternoon, the way that I would hunt for the rest of my life took a 90-degree turn.

By putting up a stand and hunting it immediately, rather than the next day or the next week, we give ourselves the best possible chance of catching hunter-wise bucks using normal, undisturbed patterns. Think of it as making your own beginner's luck!

You need to be able to do three things really well to make this approach work for you. First and foremost, you need to be able to carry a stand into the woods and put it up quickly and quietly. There are any number of ways to accomplish this. I still prefer screw-in tree steps for my own hunting due to their versatility, but I realize the physical exertion required to climb a tree in this manner is not for everyone. Sectional climbing ladders, such as API's Stackin' Stiks (as well as others), are versatile and have become very popular in recent years. You may want to check them out.

The stand you choose must go up quietly. I prefer light-weight aluminum stands for this type of hunting because they are easier to handle quietly than are heavy stands. Fixed-position stands are the best overall choice because you're not always going to find a tree that is straight enough to use a climbing stand. You can usually find one that will allow you to hang a chain-on, strap-on or pin-mounted stand. My personal preference for this type of hunting are the pin-mounted styles.

Secondly, you need to be good at flying by the seat of your pants. In some cases, you'll be choosing hunting spots with-out the benefit of any type of scouting. Fortunately, there are enough resources available, such as tracks on road crossings and field edges, aerial photos, topo maps and conversations with landowners and local residents, that you can pull this off with reasonable effectiveness. The better you become at using these resources, especially the aerial photos, the better will be your stand choices.

I'm about as dependent upon aerial photos as I am upon my bow or my treestand. Sitting at home, I can "walk" a property without exposing a single deer to my scent. All the terrain and cover that serve to funnel deer are right there in black and white. I can tell where the bedding ridges are, where the deer are most likely to feed, where the heaviest cover is (darkest areas on the photos) and where the travel routes connecting all this good stuff are located. Aerial photos are most easily obtained through the county soil conservation office in the county seat where you hunt.

Finally, you need to be good at gaining access to hunting

Highly mobile stand hunting requires specialized equipment, such as a light bow, a fanny pack, treesteps and a lightweight stand.

areas. Since you will be moving around often with this style of hunting, you'll need more ground to hunt. I realize that in some parts of the country this is a problem. Do the best you can. If you can get access to a couple of good areas your options really open up.

Whenever possible, spend some time scouting after the season in order to learn all you need to know at a time when your presence won't hurt your chances for success later. While you're at it, pick several likely stand sites. You may even choose to put a couple of stands up at this time. You're going to need some morning stands anyway, as it is nearly impossible to pick a tree and put up a stand in the darkness of predawn. You'll also run across some spots that are prime candidates for this low-impact hunting method. Jot them down in a notebook and come back during the season with a stand on your back.

Lightweight stands with pin or strap mounting systems are quiet and will go up quickly and quietly.

There is one drawback to hit-and-run stand hunting. One of the goals in low-impact hunting is to keep ground scent to a minimum, so that approaching deer won't run across it before they get to you. This means you won't have the luxury of doing a bunch of on-the-ground scouting. As a result, you're going to miss the perfect stand site from time to time. It can be frustrating to see big bucks passing out of range, but you have to consider any hunt successful when you see such animals in the first place. Besides, you'll get better at this as you go along, and you'll pull everything together often enough.

You might need to choose a tree that is more open than you normally would select, just so there will be plenty of clear shooting lanes. It is better to take small chances with concealment than to risk not getting a shot at a nice buck. Besides, you may not hunt the spot again for the rest of the season, anyway. So, don't worry if you spook a couple of does.

This is definitely a demanding hunting style, both mentally and physically. But I can't think of a better way to lower your impact. The harder you work at it, the better you'll do. When I started hunting this way, the number of big bucks I saw immediately shot up. One of my buddies calls it the "Pop-Tart strategy": you pop in, toast 'em, and pop out! Now it's about the only way I hunt. And in my opinion, it's the deadliest possible strategy for the serious trophy hunter.

CHAPTER SIX

FROM THE OUTSIDE IN: A NEW WAY TO HUNT

We've all been there. In fact, it's a classic scenario: while scouting a hunting area after the season, we come across an area torn up with huge rubs and scrapes. A nearby bedding area suggests plenty of deer will be visiting the scrapes during the rut. We only need to look the area over for a couple of minutes before we declare, "This is the spot." Stopping back in the summer, the farmer lets us know the bucks are still around. He saw them both while baling hay. The fuse is lit. By November it's gonna be dynamite.

A quick scouting trip before the season, in October, confirms our hopes. Yep, the scrapes are still there, and bigger than ever. We even clear a tree for our stand on this trip. This is going to be the year. An entire week of vacation is mentally committed to hunting the two bucks in that immediate area, with the first day spent right over that scrape–dawn 'til dusk.

On the surface it appears to be a pretty fair strategy, but look a little deeper. There are several reasons why this approach is all too often the first step toward a disappointing season. In almost every case, running straight to the hottest sign with a treestand on your back is not the best way to hunt a limited area. In fact, this may actually be the worst way.

Remember, we were heading for the scrapes on the first

morning of our vacation. For sure, we are going to get one good hunt. We'll probably see several deer—maybe more than we've ever seen from one stand before. We'll no doubt be scented by a couple on our way to the stand, and on the stand a few more will discover us—mostly does. We may see a couple of bucks from the stand (and if we're really lucky we may even shoot one). On the walk out at least one or two more deer (possibly many more) will be aware that we have passed.

It is conceivable that before we get back to our truck, half of all the deer using the area will know a man has been there. Then comes nighttime movement. At least one nice buck is likely to come past the scrape after dark. There's a fair chance he'll run across our scent trail and become a little better educated. It keeps adding up until nearly all the deer in the area know a man was there.

If we don't take a deer on that first hunt and return the next day, the process repeats itself. Only this time there are far fewer deer still moving naturally throughout the area. And those that smell our scent, either in the air or on the ground, for the second time won't be seen during daylight hours in that area for quite a while. What seemed like a great strategy has quickly unraveled, leaving us to look for a completely new area to hunt as we puzzle over the riddle of a hotspot suddenly "going cold."

Now let's look at a different approach to hunting this same location. First off, you want to keep such a great area as fresh as you can for as long as you can, but you still want to hunt it hard enough to eventually take a nice buck. There is no better way of accomplishing this goal than starting your hunting on the fringes of the area and slowly, but surely—day by day—working your way in closer to the action. In fact, some very effective deer hunters present a good argument when they suggest that you should never

The author took this big eight-pointer in 1991 by hunting along a fenceline, well away from the area's largest concentration of buck sign.

Portable stands make it easy to "move-in" on the buck. The closer you are to the end of your hunting time, the more aggressively you should attack the area's hotspots.

work your way in closer, but should keep to the fringes all season long.

In the last chapter I went over the advantages of hunting a stand only once–hit the absolute hottest spot an area has to offer–and then move on. I also mentioned that to be effective you need to hunt a large area or have access to several properties. However, if you are hunting a limited amount of ground and need to keep it productive for a whole season–or are hunting an individual buck and don't want to push him out of the area–it pays to use less force and more finesse. Last chapter was the force chapter, this is the finesse chapter. Both are good approaches when used under the right circumstances.

Getting back to the finesse: As long as we don't hunt right on top of a big buck's hottest activity areas, we can get away with more hunting pressure. Think about this a little bit, because we can take advantage of something here. By working our way into the best areas from the fringes, we can enjoy several good hunts instead of putting all our eggs in one basket for a single maxed out, hit-or-miss hunt. In the process of moving in gradually, we'll learn as we go. As a result, the stands we choose will be good ones.

Let me give you an example of how this strategy has worked for me. During the summer of 1991, I gained permission to hunt a good-looking area. I made a single pass through the property in mid-October and found a pair of huge scrapes and some big rubs down in a small bottom between two elevated bedding points. I knew it was the breeding hub for the area. I even put up a stand and sat there once in late October. The area had been torn up, but during my time on stand I saw nothing.

I had a lot of permission in that county and generally tended to hunt using the never-go-back method discussed in Chapter Five. Well, this spot was just too good to hunt once and walk away from.

The path I had to take to get to my stand was a long one, requiring that I cross several deer trails in the process. It was definitely a high-impact proposition. Instead of trying to hunt the hot sign again, I studied an aerial photo of the land, hoping to find a good travel route leading into the torn-up area—a spot that I could get to easily and hunt more than once. As I often do, I chose a thick fenceline for my stand, and after waiting more than a week for the area to settle back down, went in and hunted the spot.

The first time in the new stand I saw a nice buck running a doe in an adjacent patch of brush, but he never came my way. I left the stand up and went back the next day at noon. I saw several good bucks, and by the middle of the afternoon I had arrowed the biggest one. He had a nice rack, but to this day I have never seen a bigger-bodied deer. Estimates from several people and girth measurements put him close to 300 pounds, dressed! If I had continued to run back to those scrapes, I guarantee you such a seasoned and mature buck would have stopped using the area long before I could have arrowed him.

Most hunters have only one good area and can't afford to rest it for 10 days between hunts like I did in the last example. While hunting in another state during the 1994 season, I ran into exactly that situation. I only had permission to hunt a single 150-acre piece of property. So, I had to be careful to keep it fresh and huntable for my whole stay.

I didn't want to spook deer by scouting extensively, so I walked some field edges on the downwind side of the cover looking for density and track size. I also studied an aerial photo of the property. Without ever setting foot inside the cover I had enough information to put up two stands.

The outside-in strategy relies heavily upon observation as a means for determining the next move. Good binoculars are a wise investment.

Take advantage of low impact scouting techniques, such as walking downwind field edges, to learn as much as possible without putting any deer on red alert.

It is very risky to go right into a big buck's living room. When he runs across your scent in his "safe area" he will become more difficult to hunt in the general area.

They were both along fringe travel routes, far from what I felt was most likely the area of hottest activity.

After two days of slipping around the edges and watching, I found myself along an alfalfa field. I was very surprised to observe that deer were crossing the field during broad daylight to get to a bedding area farther up the creek bottom. The rest of this story I told you already in Chapter Four. I moved my stand into position and arrowed a big eight-pointer the next morning. In this low-impact manner, I could have hunted that single property many more days and never burned it out. Even though I arrowed a nice buck, I didn't feel like I got anywhere near the hottest areas.

The key is to keep the big bucks in the area from knowing they are being hunted for as long as you possibly can. Start with the lowest-impact stand sites you can find. They should have only two qualities. First, you need to be able to see what is going on around you–the more ground you

Road crossings are an excellent low-impact source of information. You can tell much about the number and size of the deer on the move, and which parts of your hunting area offer the most promise.

can watch the better. And second, the stand should provide a realistic chance of actually producing a shot. Each time you move your stand, move to progressively higher-impact areas. Usually, you can learn enough from the deer movement that you observe from each stand to give you a good idea where to try next.

Gauge the speed of this progression by the length of time you have to hunt. For a long hunt, move more slowly. For a short hunt, move quickly. By the end of the hunt, you should plan to be sitting over the best sign the area has to offer. Hopefully, you'll never make it that far because your tag will already be attached to a trophy.

Observation being such an important part of this hunting style, a good binocular is a great investment. Many of the deer I've taken while hunting from the outside in were seen from a distance first. Clear optics make the long hours of glassing enjoyable, and will help you to determine if what you are looking at is really a trophy worth pursuing.

You want to lay low, but you also want to put yourself in position to take a good buck. That's the balancing act I referred to earlier in the book. You'll gain a lot of satisfaction from hunting this way, because each step you take will be made with a purpose. When you succeed, you'll know why it happened. Sure, luck will still be a factor in success—it always is—but you'll know that it wasn't the only factor.

CHAPTER SEVEN

HUNTING ALL DAY

I parked my truck at 11:30 that morning and grabbed my bow, a treestand, and my fanny pack full of tree steps. It was only a 20-minute walk across private land to the edge of the big chunk of public land beyond it. I had walked through this area quickly the spring before and had seen some very impressive rubs along a stand of pine trees just inside the public ground. It was toward this spot that I headed. Being the first of November, I knew the rut would be getting into gear. The big rubs were there again, and very fresh. I was hoping the big buck that made them would make a trip along the edge of the pines some time during the evening hunt. I just didn't expect him so soon.

I was still climbing the tree with my stand when I heard him coming. He came chugging up the steep bluff with his mouth hanging open, breathing hard. It appeared as if he had already been on the move for most of the day. He was a 10-pointer in the 140 class, a buck that I would have been sorely tempted to shoot even though it was still early in the rut. But that was entirely academic as there was no way I'd be getting a shot with my bow lying on the ground! He passed 10 yards from the tree and disappeared over a rise, never slowing and never even glancing my way.

Three days later I had a much bigger buck catch me in another compromising situation, and again it was right in the middle of the day. The giant eight-pointer would have scored in the 150s, no question. I was just reaching down for the tote rope to pull my bow up when he came crunching into view. I tried several times to get the bow off the ground, but the buck just got too close, too fast. Soon he was right under me. Seeing the bow and then me, he bounded off 80 yards and stopped to look back at a sobbing hunter.

Not all of my mid-day encounters have ended in disappointment. In fact, several trophies have found their way onto my wall after showing up near my stand during times when most other hunters were getting lunch or taking a high-noon siesta. Some of the most profitable time you can spend on stand occurs during the middle of the day, especially during the rut–and even more so when the weather is cool. If you aren't out there from dawn until dark during the best part of the season, you're missing a good percentage of the day's action.

Let's follow a good buck through a typical day during the rut. Our boy spends the night nosing around in the places where does feed. He paces from one of these areas to another, looking for a doe that's in heat. Usually, shortly after daybreak, he'll follow a group of does out of their feeding area into the cover. Within an hour or two the does will all bed, and if none are close to their estrus peak, he'll quickly lose interest and be on the move again. His course may take him to another bedding area, or to a hot scrape or two located in areas where does pass after leaving the fields. This second shift rotation corresponds with mid-to-late morning, when most hunters are growing impatient, hungry or cold, and have started filtering out of the woods.

Now lets look at the rest of the buck's day. Let's assume that he finds no amorous does. He will soon bed down for a short nap, probably in one of the areas he's checking, or if he is old and wary he will likely withdraw to somewhere

Nothing increases your odds for success more than simply being out there. The hours from 10 a.m. to 2 p.m. can be some of the best when bucks are on the move during the rut. Take your lunch to the stand with you.

Winke took this nice 10-pointer with a rifle in south Texas. The buck was taken just before noon on a day following a full moon.

more secluded. After a couple of hours of much needed sleep, the buck is up again, rechecking some of the same areas that he hit earlier. Maybe he'll touch-up a scrape or two and nose around a few more bedding areas. Finally, as sunset begins to spur the doe herd into movement, our buck drifts back to the feeding areas and starts the process all over again.

Another set of conditions can also produce a flurry of midday activity. At certain times, buck movement is almost strictly nocturnal. When this is caused by clear nights with a full moon, midday activity is often intensified. It seems as if every buck is up and walking for a short time late in the morning. This was the case on a recent rifle hunt at the fabled Encinitos Ranch in south Texas. Despite the fact that the rut was heating up, daytime buck movement had slowly diminished with each day following a cold front. I saw 20 to 25 does on the third morning, but not a single buck. This was potentially perplexing, since the ranch is managed for a 1-to-1.8 buck-to-doe ratio. I should have seen many bucks. The first horns appeared at 10 a.m., precisely when my guide stopped to check on me. We quickly resumed the hunt, and within a half hour I had a nice 10-pointer on the ground. Even as we drove back to the ranch house an hour later, we were still seeing good bucks on the move. When buck movement is primarily nocturnal, you will do well to be on stand at midday.

Just because you are on stand all day doesn't mean you'll experience action all day long. Certain types of travel routes produce better during the day than others. Stands located between bedding and feeding areas are distinctly different from those located between two bedding areas. During most times of the year, stands on travel routes between two bedding areas would be dead, but during the rut these are the places to find maximum midday

Bedding-to-Bedding travel routes

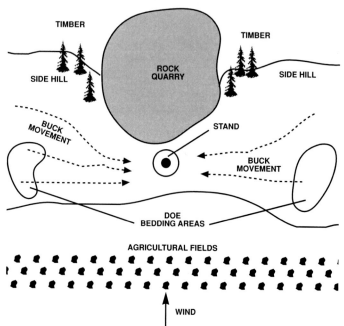

During the middle of the day, bucks are likely to use travel routes that connect two doe bedding areas. A giant eight-pointer caught the author at this location just as he reached down to pull his bow up into the tree.

movement. It's been my experience that you'll see fewer bucks on bedding to feeding trails during the early phases of the rut than on travel routes between two (or more) bedding areas.

While hunting bedding-to-bedding buck travel corridors I see many bucks, but rarely a doe. However, most of the time these areas go completely dead about an hour before sunset, and take at least an hour to heat up in the morning. By their nature, most of these stands are also in areas that will allow me to access them easily without

Bedding-to-Feeding travel routes

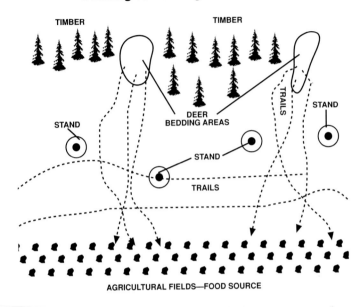

Travel routes located between bedding and feeding areas can produce fast action on bucks during the rut, but often it takes place right at sunrise and sunset. Getting to and from these stands without alarming deer is the hard part.

the risk of spooking deer before first light or when leaving after dark.

Basically, you are looking for stand sites that are located in any type of funnel between two heavily-used bedding areas. Also, in areas with broken terrain, I try to find a topographical feature that I know bucks will use in a predictable manner. I've mentioned funnels in past chapters (and I'll go into more detail in the next chapter), but they offer the best bet for action. The ideal bedding-to-bedding stand site is located back in the woods, where little exposure is required for the oldest, smartest bucks to move about.

Even the less secure, more exposed travel routes, such as a fence line, are often used at midday in areas where hunting pressure is light.

You won't find a lot of buck sign along bedding-to-bedding travel corridors because bucks only use them to get from point A to point B, and don't mess around much along the way. You'll almost never find a trail, maybe some kicked up leaves if you're lucky, so don't be fooled by the lack of sign. Trust your instincts and set up a stand. At first you may feel silly, but thereafter the bucks you see will keep you on the edge of your fold-out seat for entire days at a time.

One nice feature of midday travel routes is their ease of access. They are not near feeding areas, which means that you can get to and from them in the dark without educating any deer. As long as the wind blows your scent into areas that don't contain deer during the day, your stand set-up will permit almost surgical precision and efficiency.

Here are a couple of examples of midday bedding-to-bedding stand sites that have worked well for me in the past. One of my favorites is a stand that I have in a wooded fence line between a corn field and a large patch of idle farmland field. It connects three wooded points with a 200-acre woodlot. Deer, of course, bed heavily on these wooded points, and the woodlot serves as home for eight to 10 more does. As long as the wind blows my scent out into one of the fields, I almost never have a deer catch me on stand. I shot a dandy there several years ago, three hours before sunset.

Another classic stand that I've used several times overlooks a large rock quarry. The quarry cuts deep into the side of a gradual slope, leaving just 100 yards of cover between its top lip and the field edge above. Any deer traveling the sidehill between the bedding areas on either side of the quarry must pass through the funnel on top,

By dressing warm, you can increase the enjoyment of long hours on stand. Boot Blankets and Hand Blankets are great accessories for keeping your extremities warm.

often within bow range, and always within gun range. I only hunt the spot when the wind is carrying my scent out over the quarry. I can climb up the slope along the quarry's edge to get into my stand completely undetected. That stand has produced plenty of midday action through the years.

Seeing the effectiveness of midday hunting and actually staying out there all day are two different matters. Spending the whole day on one stand is very tedious business. Just a couple of days of this type of hunting can drive me stir crazy. I remember a hunt I went on in Manitoba several years ago. It was the last week of October and it was starting to get cold in the Interlake Region. I spent four and a half days sitting from dawn until dusk before I saw the only buck of the trip. I had seen a grand total of three does prior to that. I spent every daylight minute of my six-day hunt on stand. By the time I got back to the Midwest I was too burned out to even think about hunting . . . at least for a couple of days!

Big, comfortable treestands with padded bench-style seats make long hours on stand more bearable.

If you don't have the patience to sit all day on one stand—and few hunters do—then consider moving to a different stand late in the morning. This can break up the monotony and give stiff muscles a chance to loosen up. It is also a great time to spot check for buck sign around a couple of other stands for future reference. Just don't delay too long, because good action may be passing you by.

The right clothing for maximum warmth will help you stay out there for extended periods. I have a few tips that have worked well for me. Find a good pair of loose fitting insulated bib overalls with zip-up leg openings. Carry these, along with your other outerwear, when walking to your stand. This will keep you from sweating, which will in turn help you stay much warmer once you get settled. You can pull the overalls easily over your boots once you get to your destination. Tie-on hand muffs are great for keeping your hands warm. Dry, air-activated hand warmers can be used in many ways to keep you cozy, including sandwiched between two inner clothing layers. Eat a well-balanced breakfast and carry a good lunch with you. Just as a motor requires fuel to run, your body burns calories to keep you warm.

Persistence is one of the most critical qualities that a would-be trophy hunter must cultivate. Always keep in mind that with big bucks, it only takes one deer to change your whole season. A big buck can show up at any time. You may be sitting on stand, convinced that there isn't a good buck within miles, and 10 seconds later you may be drawing your bow or shouldering your gun on the biggest buck you've ever seen. Time spent on good stands is what it's all about, and every minute on stand brings you one minute closer to seeing a big buck.

CHAPTER EIGHT

READING THE TERRAIN

When I set up the stand three and a half weeks earlier, there had been nothing to suggest the perfect place to put it. No rubs, no tracks and no scrapes. In fact, there was very little about the wide bench in the pastured woods that would indicate any whitetails were even using the area at all, let alone the big buck that I had set my sights on. The only thing I had going for me was the lay of the land. The terrain suggested that the area was a natural travel route, and with blind faith, I stuck my stand in a tree.

I sat there only once that fall before taking a nice buck somewhere else. During that one day I saw three Pope & Young class bucks from it, though. The following November, my friend Dan Knasel came in from Michigan to hunt with me, so I turned the stand over to him. Two hours after sunrise a beautiful 10-point buck made his cautious way toward the excited hunter. As the buck passed 20 yards away, Dan drew his bow and sent an arrow directly into the buck's vitals. After a short burst, the buck was down and the woods were again still, save for my friend's rapid breathing. Dan's stand paid off because I had been able to read the terrain in that area to predict where a buck would likely travel.

Today's deer hunters are well aware of the many forms of sign that deer leave, and all too often that is the only thing they look for when scouting a new stand area. Interpreting tracks, trails, scrapes, and rubs will provide plenty of details, but sign alone is not enough to solve the puzzle of a big buck's travel patterns. When they are on the move, especially during the rut, bucks leave little sign. Rarely will they use trails with the same consistency that does will, and the rubs and scrapes they made in October near their core areas are often completely abandoned as the rut draws near.

Only one factor in the trophy buck's otherwise unpredictable behavior is even remotely constant throughout the season, regardless of where you hunt him. Bucks always use the terrain to their strict advantage whenever they travel. That's a fact you can stake your hunting season on. I do it every year.

Bucks that have mastered the survival game don't skyline themselves unnecessarily, at least not for long. How many times have you seen a good buck cross an open field along the top of a hill? It almost never happens, but if you take a careful look at the tracks left in a shallow swale in the same area, you'll probably see some whoppers. How would you travel through an area if you were trying to remain unseen? That's exactly what the biggest bucks will do.

Trophy bucks also take the path of least resistance whenever they can. Deer, in general, are pretty lazy. They prefer the easy route. Rarely will they work any harder than they have to when going from point A to point B. Granted, bucks aren't as devoted to this calling as does, which almost blindly follow the easiest course, but they still display a tendency to avoid difficult travel. Many times knowing where a buck won't go will lead you directly to where he will.

I took advantage of this fact when setting up one of my stands during the 1994 season. It was one of those situations where I just went into an area cold and put up a stand. One of my favorite tactics when doing this is to study the terrain and pick my stand sites accordingly. I'll almost completely ignore the buck sign that I run across when setting up this

Learning to read the affect terrain has on buck movement can result in some dandy bucks taken during the rut. The author and hunting buddies took these in early November, 1993.

way. It is just too tough to unravel all that sign and keep your ground scent to an acceptably low level at the same time. You can cut through all the confusion and get right down to business by relying primarily on the terrain.

I wound up with my stand 30 yards from the brink of a very steep and high bluff that overlooked a beautiful bend in the river far below. It was one of the most enjoyable spots I've ever hunted. A presumed bedding ridge fed right into the stand area from another angle. Anything traveling that ridge, or sneaking along the top of the bluff, would be sandwiched right between my stand and the edge of the steep drop-off.

A monstrous nontypical with double drop tines—one of the biggest bucks I've ever had within bow range—came right along the edge of the bluff. Instead of continuing past my stand as I knew he must, he stopped in a thin patch of brush only 30 yards away for several minutes before dropping over the edge of the nearly vertical slope. Even as I watched it happen, I knew it was a fluke, and even though I didn't get him, he displayed a tendency to follow the terrain that very nearly put him in my freezer. That buck was lucky, but I could tell you about several others encountered at similar stands that weren't.

If you can find the path of least resistance that also satisfies the big buck's need for security, you have found a good place to ambush him. Basically, sign is of secondary concern. Of course, the location has to connect two points that the buck has some interest in traveling between. For example, he may be moving back and forth between feeding and bedding areas early and late in the season, or between two bedding areas used by does during the rut. If a buck is traveling through a general area, knowing how he is likely to use the terrain found there is the key to having him right in your lap.

Saddles and draws represent easy travel routes to deer. Draws extending into fields offer low profile travel for bucks as they stage and head to feed, and also when crossing the same fields later during the rut. By taking your stand on the downwind side of the draw you have a good chance of catching the biggest buck as he waits in "security" for the cover of darkness before venturing out to feed.

Saddles are another super ambush spot. They are often found within the cover of the woods, and present an easy point for the buck to crest a rise without skylining himself. A saddle doesn't have to be very deep to pull in traveling deer. When you find a good one, hunt it sparingly until the rut kicks in, then sit all day.

Bluffs (as described in the last example of the big nontypical) or very steep sections of a sidehill will cause deer that normally follow mid-slope contours to detour from their routes and funnel either to the top or the bottom of the slope, making at least one excellent stand site. Also, cut into many steep hillsides there is a more gradual slope, often in the form

October rubs, such as this one, are poor indicators of what bucks will be doing during the rut. Sign is less important than the lay of the land when predicting buck movement.

of a dry wash, that deer use for ascending and descending the more vertical sections. The farther it is between these easy grades, the better will be the odds that a nice buck will use the one you're watching.

Creeks and rivers have a fairly obvious affect on buck travel patterns. All deer will most likely cross the flow at its most shallow sections. There will be heavy trails in these places, especially if each crossing is widely separated by long stretches of deeper water. Though they don't seem to like to be confined to tight travel areas, big bucks also use these crossings. Floating in a canoe during the summer is a good way to find well-used crossings.

In areas with rugged terrain, there are usually steep washouts that run from the top of the hillside down to the bottom. Depending upon how deep and steep the sides of these ditches are, this terrain feature can have a great impact on deer movement. At the very least, there will be two places where deer traveling the sidehill can cross the ditch with ease, the top and the bottom. Often, there are points in between that are also used regularly. Ditches are one of the first things I look for when scouting a new block of broken country for likely stand locations.

Big bucks use ridges differently than the rest of the deer herd. Most often they will not travel the very top of the ridge as will does and smaller bucks. They prefer to stay 40 to 50 yards, sometimes farther, down the slope while paralleling the ridge top, usually on the downwind side. In this way they can keep track of what is happening on top without exposing themselves to danger.

Often, bucks will bed on the points that jut from ridges, using the sidehill travel routes to enter and exit these areas. It can be tough to determine exactly where they travel along the slope, since in most places there are not enough of them to leave a trail. Sometimes rub lines will reveal the route, but at others you will simply have to rely upon your instincts. One of the rare times that big bucks will actually travel the top of a ridge is when it is very broad, or when they are trailing a hot doe during the rut.

The author took this nice eight-pointer in early November, 1994. The buck was following a break in the terrain when he passed within 25 yards. There was very little buck sign in the area.

Creek crossings are classic terrain features that bucks use in a very predictable manner when on the move. When there are few crossings, those that exist will be used heavily.

A high ground swamp crossing, such as a beaver dam or a ridge between two low areas, is an excellent stand location. Deer will stream through such a place in an effort to avoid the muck. Another similar terrain feature is a large pond or lake. The upwind side produces a unique opportunity in which you can intercept deer passing along the water's edge with no fear of being scented. By the same token, deer follow the banks of deep, sluggish streams and rivers for considerable distances. In fact, any structure that breaks up the land, and runs in approximately the same direction the deer wish to go, will be used as a travel route.

Sometimes man-made terrain features are the best kind. The big eight-pointer that got away from me in 1993 (described in the last chapter) was using a sidehill travel route but had to work his way to the top of the slope to get around a large limestone quarry that had been cut deeply into the slope many years before. Such spots are few and far between, but when you find them you have a gold mine that will produce big buck action year after year.

Just finding a likely terrain feature isn't enough. Remember, there has to be a reason for Mr. Big to be traveling through the area in the first place. If the location you are thinking about is not sandwiched between two places where bucks like to be, you may as well keep right on looking for one that is.

Hunting pressure during the gun season will dictate the types of locations that have the best chance of producing shots during those times. As big bucks attempt to elude other hunters, they head for thick cover and out-of-the-way places. In some cases, they even leave classic deer cover to take refuge in small overlooked patches. My buddies and I have had excellent results taking big bucks in classic pheasant cover after they exited the big woods areas that other deer hunters typically concentrate on. Anticipate these movements and watch locations that allow the buck to keep a low profile as he heads for safety. These spots will produce consistent action on opening morning, year after year.

Big bucks are different from other deer, and the types of places they use when traveling is one of the primary ways they differ. Reading the terrain can really up your odds on trophy bucks.

CHAPTER NINE

ADVANCED WIND STRATEGIES

It was one of those frigid early November days. Tom Weighner didn't want to sit in one of his ridge stands, exposed to the 20 mph winds, so he slipped down into the valley below his house. At least here he would find some shelter from the blast. What he also found was an incredible snarl of monster buck sign. With three hours of daylight left, the bowhunter crawled up into a fallen oak top on the downwind side of a good trail and waited.

An hour later he got a weird feeling and, turning, was jolted to see a huge eight-pointer with a two-foot spread loping across a clearing straight toward him. Blowing 90 degrees to the direction the buck was moving, the wind was perfect. Tom got ready. Things stayed perfect only until the next gust. The swirling currents took Tom's scent right to the buck, who wasted no time in swapping ends.

How many stories like Tom's do you have? Obviously, there is more to playing the wind than just setting up a stand on the prevailing downwind side of the sign you are watching. We can't control the wind, but we can recognize what makes it do what it does. And we can find stands that allow us to use the wind to our advantage. Maybe just as importantly, we can also realize which situations will only cause spooked game and ruined hunts.

Think of wind flowing over the terrain as if it were water

over a creek bed. When flowing water runs into still pockets it begins to swirl, creating an eddy. The faster the mainstream flow, the more violent and unpredictable the swirling. This is how the wind acts when it encounters a protected pocket of calm air. It swirls, and the more gusty the wind, the more unpredictable the result. Learn to anticipate how the wind will swirl in these protected areas and you'll increase your odds of killing big whitetails.

In the case of a narrow draw or ravine, the wind will strike the far (downwind) slope and be turned downward, actually blowing in the opposite direction across the bottom of the draw. That situation ruined my hunts on more than one occasion before I realized what was happening. If you are planning to set up a stand on the bottom of a draw, anticipate a lot of swirling, maybe even a reversal of the wind direction.

The wind reacts differently in broad valleys than it does in narrow ones. When the wind strikes the upslope of a broad valley, it will be pushed upward instead of pulled downward. This situation can have some very interesting applications, as this story illustrates. I had gotten permission for my friend, Greg, to hunt on a great piece of whitetail property. On one part of the farm there was a pond that was torn up with sign. It was right at the head of a draw, so all the cover was located on the downhill side of the pond's levee.

We picked a tree along the edge of the woods, below the dike. The wind was blowing from the woods to the pond, which wasn't a concern because we figured any large bucks would be cruising just inside the cover below the pond waiting for does to come out. Greg was positioned right along the edge of the woods, about 15 yards below the levee, with his stand roughly even with its top.

Carry a container of wind-testing powder whenever you are out scouting a new hunting area. Talcum powder works fine. Stop often to check the swirling winds so you can anticipate the best conditions for hunting the area.

Without warning, a nice 10-pointer strolled out onto the dike, catching the bowhunter flat-footed. The buck passed dead downwind of Greg without even hesitating or raising his nose. For other reasons, the shot never materialized, but an important lesson was reinforced. Even though he and the buck were at the same level, Greg's scent was blown right up over the buck's head. The wind was actually blowing parallel to the slope, carrying Greg's scent well over the buck. I've successfully used this knowledge several times in tight situations. It is just one more trick that can pay off big under the right conditions.

Wind will funnel when it flows in the same direction as the lay of the land. For instance, I pointed out how the wind will reverse itself when it blows 90 degrees to a steep draw. But, if it blows at an angle to the draw, it will be funneled to follow the terrain. Along the bottom, the wind will actually be blowing parallel to the draw. You can use this knowledge in two ways.

First, due to the unpredictability of the swirling winds, you should stay out of bottom land stands as much as possible. Rutting bucks will leave sign galore in these places, making it tough to walk away. But sometimes that is simply the best strategy. When things are not perfect, it is very easy to get blown out by every deer in the area. Second, if you really need to hunt a hotspot down in a draw, only do it when the wind is light and steady, and then only if it is blowing in the same direction as the draw so its direction will be consistent.

One of the best stand locations in rugged terrain is on a ridge or along the top of a steep slope. By hanging to the downwind edge, without going too far over the rim, your scent will blow out over the trees and away from the noses of deer. With a stand in such a location, deer can approach literally from any direction and not smell you. But, if you get too far down over the top of the slope your scent will be pushed downward instead of blown out over the bottoms. Typically, if your treestand is high enough so you can see over the crest, your scent will go out instead of down.

Using the stream analogy and some common sense, it's possible to anticipate how the wind will swirl around a proposed stand. In a pinch, your best guess will have to do, but it is much better to spend some time scouting the area right after the season. At this time the vegetation and prevailing winds will most closely duplicate the conditions found during the hunting season. A tube of wind-testing

The author's hunting buddy, Dan Knasel, took this buck as it passed 20 yards downwind of his stand. Because the stand was high and the ground fell away in the direction of the deer, the bowhunter's scent remained above the buck's head.

powder, or something similar, carried while scouting will be invaluable in determining localized wind swirls, and will tell you what is likely to happen to your scent in that area. Try to figure out why the wind is flowing the way it is so you can learn as you go. This understanding will pay off in the future.

Knowing where your scent is being blown as you approach your stand is important too. Scout this out as well. I'm a firm believer that every well-chosen stand should produce some type of action. If it doesn't, more than likely I did something wrong, and botching my entry is one of the biggies.

Not only does terrain affect wind direction, but so does cover. As the wind moves through thick cover, it slows down, pulling faster moving air in its direction. What this means to you as a hunter is that the amount of cover at

Wind blowing over a ravine

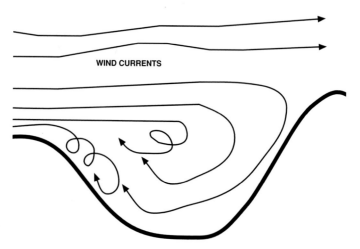

When the wind blows over a narrow ravine it will actually be reversed, blowing in the opposite direction along the bottom. When it gusts, swirling winds result, spreading your scent all through the area.

stand level and below will affect how far your scent is blown before it is low enough for a deer to smell. This element of stand placement is more important to the bowhunter than to the gun hunter because of the relatively short distances involved.

Heavy cover will slow the wind more than light cover, and cause your scent to swirl to the ground quickly, maybe within 10 yards of an 18-foot-high stand. Early season hunting, with its heavy foliage, requires that you pay particular attention to this fact. In heavy cover, any deer that's downwind, no matter how close to your tree, may catch a whiff of your scent.

On the other hand, thin cover will slow the wind down little, creating the least amount of swirling. In the best case,

Wind blowing against an upslope

WIND CURRENTS

STAND

WIND CURRENTS ARE LIFTED UP AT TOP OF SLOPE. DEER LOCATED IN THIS AREA WILL NOT SCENT HUNTER IN TREESTAND PLACED AS SHOWN.

When the wind is blowing into an upslope, it lifts over the top lip, creating a situation where a deer can walk close to the top of the ridge and not smell you, even though you are in a treestand at eye level with the animal. This can give you an edge when setting up stands to cover a wide travel corridor.

with your treestand 20 feet off the ground, you may be able to position yourself as much as 20 to 25 yards upwind of a deer crossing and not be scented. You can use this strategy to cover wide travel routes more effectively with your bow. Instead of placing your stand all the way on the downwind edge, move it upwind as far as you dare. Deer will pass downwind of your stand without scenting you, and you can cover twice as much woods, doubling your chances of having a buck pass within range.

Gusting winds are the hardest to hunt. Not only are smart old bucks leery of these conditions, but if you are hunting any type of broken terrain at all, the effects of gusting are impossible to predict. As the gusts ebb and flow in

Wind blowing at an angle to ravine

TOP OF SLOPE

WIND CURRENTS

TOP OF SLOPE

RAVINE

When the wind blows at an angle to a steep ravine, it will be funneled to follow the direction of the contours. When the wind is steady, this situation will permit you to hunt down in the ravine and still control the dispersal of your scent. However, when the wind gusts, all bets are off.

Wind blowing through vegetation

WIND CURRENTS

When blowing through heavy vegetation, the wind swirls more than when blowing through open vegetation. Therefore, if your tree is relatively sparse, and you are at least 15-18 feet off the ground, you can set up your stand as much as 20 yards upwind of where you expect deer to pass and not be detected.

hilly topography, they create a kind of back and forth movement of the air. It doesn't take long before your scent is spread out all over the place. I don't have any answers to this problem. When it's gusty, I simply stay away from my better stands, or hunt from ones located in very flat areas. Though my chances of seeing a good buck are low in some of these spots, at least I'm hunting without fouling up any good areas.

Big bucks don't always travel with the wind in their faces. In fact, in the past several years I've paid particular attention to the direction deer were moving relative to the wind. I am simply amazed by the number of quality bucks (and mature does for that matter) that I see traveling with the wind directly at their backs during daylight hours.

I believe there are two reasons why I see quite a few of these seemingly suicidal bucks. First, I go well out of my way to hunt deer that aren't being hunted by anyone else. Second, I move around a lot. If the buck has been traveling a certain route often and never senses danger, I think he becomes a bit overconfident. But let him smell your scent there one time, even after dark, and I guarantee you that he won't come strolling in with the wind at his back again!

Because of the types of places that I hunt, I'll often set up with the expectation of having a buck walk past with the wind at his back, but a better strategy for the average hunting area is one in which the wind is almost perfect for the buck, but not quite. In most hunted whitetail cover, it is tough to get a big buck to walk anywhere with the wind at his back. But, he feels very secure when quartering into the wind, and will move readily under these conditions. You can use that to your advantage.

By learning to master the wind, you can negate a buck's greatest defense–his sense of smell. Do that, and you're well on your way to consistently tagging him.

The author arrowed this 10-pointer in 1990. Using only his voice, he called the buck from 150 yards away right to the base of his tree. A deer's ability to home in on the exact source of a sound is phenomenal.

and quietly become a part of the woods and await your opportunity.

However, when you have lots of ground to hunt, you can afford to be more aggressive. Look at the hunters who specialize in rattling up big bucks down in Texas. On a big ranch, you can rattle and move and rattle and move–all day long–until you contact that one big boy that's in the right frame of mind to come on in. So what if you educate a few bucks along the way. There's plenty of room and lots more bucks where they came from. Under these conditions, blind calling, and lots of it, is a good strategy. Gary Roberson, owner of Texas-based Burnham Brothers Game Calls, has been rattling up bucks in the Lone Star State for nearly three decades.

"On ranches with buck-to-doe ratios of one buck to four does (or narrower), rattling will produce good results," says Roberson. "The bucks must be competitive. I remember rattling up one buck that came in at a run. He was a real fighter. Every point on his rack was broken off! Each deer has a personality. Only the more aggressive bucks will respond to rattling in this way, others will slip in on the downwind side, still others won't respond at all.

"I like to start rattling as early as the middle of October, but the best action is in the end of November down here. I'll change my calling style to match the conditions. Early in the season I'll do more ticking of the tines to simulate sparring. Later I'll rattle very aggressively. People who hunt with me are amazed at how hard I go at it, but I've found that the more aggressive I am the more aggressive the buck will be. I recommend rattling in pairs with a hunter and a caller. Always continue rattling until the buck is in range, because if you stop, he'll stop. Stay hidden by trying to rattle behind a bush or some other type of cover, and try to keep your hands and the horns hidden. I once had a buck jump right into a bush with me! I had to bend over to protect myself!"

In a typical day, Gary will walk and rattle over a large area. In good spots he'll wait half an hour, otherwise about 15 minutes. On his very best day, he rattled up twelve bucks before noon! To Roberson, the setup is critical. "When I'm rattling for a bowhunter, I'll set the hunter across a small opening downwind from me," says Roberson. "Bucks will try to circle the clearing to catch my scent and run into the hunter. When a buck locks up, I'll grunt to him. If he locks up again, I'll stick one antler above the brush so he can see it. Murray Burnham taught me that trick many years ago."

While moving and rattling is surely the ultimate way to present your calling to the maximum number of bucks, few of us outside of Texas or the Canadian prairies (and to a lesser extent, the plains states) have access to enough ground to make that work. Most of us are calling from tree-

An effective setup for rattling

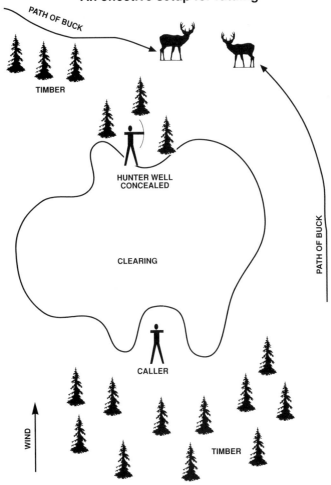

You can take advantage of a buck's tendency to circle downwind when coming to the call by hunting in tandem. The caller sets up directly up- wind of a small clearing, while the hunter conceals himself directly downwind and waits for a close-range shot.

stands and rarely get down and move to a new spot after each sequence. Stan Potts, of central Illinois, has rattled up some monsters. In fact, Stan's personal best, a huge 11-pointer that netted 195⅝ P & Y points as a typical, was rattled in back in 1983, at a time when few hunters outside of Texas were doing much rattling. His giant buck could well be the biggest buck ever rattled in by a bowhunter.

"It was the day after the first gun season had ended," says Potts. "November 21st, to be exact. I got to my stand at about 2:30 in the afternoon, and at 3:00 I rattled for about 30 seconds and then hung my antlers up. I heard a sound and looked to see a squirrel. I turned away and heard another sound from the same direction. I just figured it was him again. When I looked back you can imagine my shock when the biggest buck I've ever seen was standing there only 50 yards away. He was all dark and blown up, with his hair standing straight up. The giant buck dropped his head and started walking toward a thicket.

"I knew there were only two trails through the thicket, and when he came into the open again he would be either 20 yards away or 40 yards away. I turned into position and got ready. He was on the 20 yard trail. He went behind a red haw tree and I drew my bow. He stopped behind the tree and all I could see was the buck's nose. A few seconds later he was walking again. When he stepped out he was quartering away and was also sharply downhill from me, so I aimed high and back to hit his vitals. On the release the arrow sunk to the fletching right where I was aiming. That's when I started really getting nervous. I began second guessing myself. 'Did I shoot too far back?' But I knew it was a good hit. After only about five or 10 minutes I climbed down and went back to town for help.

"A couple of buddies came back with me after dark to trail the monster. We found decent blood for about 50

Illinois bowhunter Stan Potts rattled in this giant and took him with an arrow. Not surprisingly, more than a decade later, Potts is still a firm believer in rattling. The buck had a net typical score of 195⅜ Pope and Young points.

It is possible to call too much. Big bucks like to circle when they come in to a call. If they get downwind and scent you, the chances of getting a crack at the deer in that same area in the future are extremely low.

yards, but with the high entry angle and no exit hole, almost all the bleeding was internal. We lost the blood in a grass field. I started to circle back toward where the buck had come from, shining the flashlight out in front of me. That's when I saw a huge antler sticking up above the grass. He had only gone about 125 yards, and had died seconds after the arrow hit him."

Today, Stan Potts still does a lot of rattling during the rut. "I wouldn't think of going hunting without my horns," he said. "I start rattling about the last week of October. I think the pre-rut and right after the peak are the best times to rattle.

"I don't do anything special. I don't think its possible to actually imitate the sounds of two bucks fighting, but you really don't have to. They come to it anyway. I smack the horns together hard when I start a sequence, just to get the attention of any bucks within hearing range. I rattle for about 1½ minutes and then quickly hang the horns up and grab my bow. I wait 15 minutes and then rattle for another 30 seconds or so. I might wait another hour before starting another sequence. I rattle all day long while I'm on stand. I also keep a grunt call handy to call to bucks that hang up out of range when coming to the rattling."

Stan admitted that his success rate is not overly high. "I call in a buck maybe one out of every 15 to 20 times that I rattle. Most of those are subordinates. But every once in awhile I'll bring in a real dandy. I also like to rattle to deer that I see passing out of range because I feel rattling can be heard farther away than grunt calls."

Calling is a personal decision. You sure don't have to call to take trophy bucks. On the other hand, if the conditions permit, there is no reason not to. If only one wallhanger is tagged in your hunting lifetime directly as a result of rattling or grunting, it is well worth the effort.

CHAPTER ELEVEN

PUTTING IT ALL TOGETHER: A CLASSIC HUNT

During the 1995 season, I had a hunt that produced a giant buck and brought to light many of the things I've written about in this book. It should serve as a good example of how the process of trophy hunting works from start to finish.

I was hunting a new area that year. It was a large block of ground that holds a lot of deer and some really good bucks. Years of searching for the best possible areas within my home state of Iowa had brought me to this particular farm. I had the benefit of only two days of scouting during the spring, with only a couple of stands going up as a result. As the bow season rolled around, I was just one step removed from going in cold.

Due to heavy spring rains, only two crop fields had been planted on the property; both were in soybeans. In early October, I began hunting one of those fields.

EARLY SEASON FEEDING PATTERNS

I started by hanging back on the downwind edge to get a look at what was coming out, and where. The second evening, I slipped into a better position. From there I saw several bucks, but a couple of them really caught my eye. They were both dandies–bucks that would push Boone and

Crockett minimums. I immediately began hunting those two deer.

Regardless of where they came out, it appeared as if all the bucks were passing within bow range of several trees that jutted out from the edge of the woods. The next evening I moved closer to those trees, but high winds kept the deer under wraps. The tension grew as the week rolled on. I was able to hunt the stand several more times without seeing either of the two bucks. Finally satisfied that I had things pretty well figured out, I moved to a tree that offered the best possible chance for getting a shot should one of the bruisers come out. It had taken me five evenings to narrow it down, but now I was ready.

Three evenings later I got my chance. Twenty minutes before sunset, the does began to gather in a grassy area next to the wood line. If events followed the normal routine, the does would munch on the clipped hay grass for awhile and then line out past my stand and into the bean field. Any bucks that came out would eventually follow them. I only hoped one of the giants would be among them.

The wind had been good all evening, but now it began to blow from the woods straight out into the field. The does would have to pass directly downwind of me on their way to feed. I held my breath as the first group of six does started past. They were close, and I hoped my scent would blow over their heads. I guess they weren't close enough. Catching a whiff of my scent, the lead doe jumped and stiff-legged it back toward the rest of the group. Soon all the does and fawns in the grassy opening were watching the nervous doe. As long as she didn't blow I was still all right.

One of the giant bucks picked that exact moment to step out of the woods and begin cropping grass. He was better than 100 yards away, but my binocular revealed each long tine on his wide, 10-point rack. He paid little attention to the does despite their tense body language. Soon he was joined

The author missed a buck because he couldn't clearly see his sight pins. Make sure your pins or crosshairs are visible throughout legal shooting time.

by several lesser bucks. Now I had three distinct groups of deer waiting to pass my tree. They were strung out for 125 yards down the narrow strip of short grass. It reminded me of jets lined up in the queue for landing at Chicago O'Hare.

There was plenty of daylight left. *This still has a chance,* I thought.

The first group of does again started heading carefully toward my scent stream. I had done everything possible to eliminate my scent. I only hoped it would be enough. Again, the lead doe locked up and turned back. This time she stamped the ground and blew loudly. Now she had everyone's undivided attention, including the big buck's. The group milled for another 15 minutes. During that entire time the big buck never once took his eyes off the doe.

Obviously, she hadn't gotten a real strong hit of my scent—or maybe the beans were just too tempting. Either way, with only five minutes of shooting time remaining, she was again headed my way. Just as before, she hit the scent stream and froze, only this time she bounded forward instead of back, taking the whole group with her. This was the signal the second group of does had been waiting for. They immediately lined out and walked briskly past my tree, not showing any signs of scenting me. Seventy-five yards behind the does, the big buck was now heading my way at a steady walk!

With only minutes of legal time remaining, the buck began to pass through the narrow shooting lane, where I waited for him at full draw. The 20-yard shot should have been a piece of cake. I was excited, but not overly. *Why can't I get the pin on him,* I thought.

When I focused on the buck I couldn't see my sight pin, and when I focused on the pins I couldn't clearly see the buck. The whole time he was walking slowly through my shooting lane, perfectly broadside. My peep sight had cut down the amount of light that reached my eye until what should have been an easy shot had turned into a five second

The buck that was eventually bagged on November 7 was first grunted almost to within bow range on November 4 before hitting Winke's scent trail and spooking.

nightmare. As I focused on the 20 yard pin, I saw movement enter the peep sight from the direction the buck was approaching. It was now or never. I punched the trigger. "THWACK."

Why wasn't the buck running? It never occurred to me that I might miss. In fact it took several seconds before the realization struck home. He stood there perfectly broadside in my shooting lane, staring up at me. He hadn't been scratched! I had blown it!

Scrambling, I tried to get another arrow on the string before the buck got away. I never made it. Even as I came to full draw he was stiff-legging out of my shooting lane.

For several days afterwards I kicked myself until I was finally able to resolve things. My mistake had been glaring. I had always shot at walking bucks without trying to stop them, reasoning that when they stopped they might not be exactly in one of my typically narrow shooting lanes. With the light fading fast, I should have whistled or grunted to hold him as I took the needed time to get everything lined up. There was enough light for a good shot, but not enough for a quick one.

TRAVEL ROUTE TACTICS DURING THE RUT

My next real action came two weeks later, after hunting several days in Illinois and then returning to the soybean field. Nothing was happening there, so I decided I'd try a new area.

The day dawned clear, cold and still with lots of frost. It was the perfect morning for every buck on the property to be moving. By 9:15 I had seen several bucks, including a 140s-class 10-pointer, and something bigger that I couldn't clearly make out. Both had been out of range, and did nothing more than stop momentarily to look in my direction when I grunted at them.

I was beginning to think about climbing down when I saw a buck standing along the edge of the woods about 150 yards away. He had plenty of mass but his head was down and I couldn't tell anything about his tines. He wasn't overly wide, either. I wasn't even sure he was a keeper until he raised his head and looked to the side. My eyes must have doubled in size as the Leica binocular clearly revealed a wall of long tines on each thick beam.

Up until then I had been fairly detached, but now I was tearing at my chest pocket for the grunt call. With my heart racing, I watched for a few moments to see which direction he would go before I called. His first step was away from me. "Uuurrrp." Nothing. It would need to be louder. "URRRRPP!" He stopped and looked my way. Another softer grunt got him started. He came walking slowly along the edge of the trees, heading straight for my stand. I was absolutely confident that I had him. By now I should know better than to think that way!

Still 75 yards away, the buck began to circle out into the chest-high foxtail grass that grew in the small field in front of me. That was okay. He would still be forced, by a thin line of brush across the field, to come within 25 yards. The wind was perfect. Things looked great until the buck hit my entry trail. I had slipped through the foxtail that morning, believing the center of the field to be the least likely place that a buck would approach from. Surely they would work along the edge of the thin band of trees. Wrong!

He locked up for only 10 to 15 seconds before blowing loudly and bolting 50 yards in the opposite direction. He stopped, and steam issued from his nostrils as he blew again. By the time he was out of sight I was sick. I wanted to tumble forward out of the stand and end it all right there!

After continuing to work the area around the bean field for two more days, I again decided to try the long finger of brush. I pulled out my aerial photos at noon on the 6th of November and chose a spot about 400 yards from where the buck had hit my scent trail two days before. I knew the wind would be perfect for the spot the next morning, so I quickly snuck in and put up a stand. Leaving the spot, I went back to the bean field that evening.

Daybreak on November 7 found me 20 feet off the ground watching the long finger. I planned to stay on stand all day long. Much like it had the previous time I hunted this area, the day dawned cool, crisp and frosty. I hadn't been on the stand more than 10 minutes when I heard the distinct sound of a buck grunting, and saw a form dashing along the far side of the finger. Directly opposite me, probably only 30 yards away, the buck stopped and peered intently into the cover. I couldn't make out antlers yet and didn't want to risk pulling my binocular up. After a few moments, the buck put his head down and dove into the cover, crashing back in the direction he had come.

I knew from his behavior that the buck was cutting off a doe that was trying to use the finger to get to a large block of connected timber 100 yards beyond my stand. Does usually win such contests eventually, so I expected to see that buck again. Twenty minutes later, right after the start of legal shooting time, I saw the doe coming straight down the middle of the finger. I didn't move as first one buck, and then a second, showed up 30 yards behind her. The first buck was a 130s eight-pointer and the second was much bigger. I didn't try to size him up; one glance told me was better than big enough. It appeared as if the doe would bring him right past for an easy shot.

It took only two seconds for everything to unravel. The doe turned from her ideal course, and then stopped right under my stand. I'm sure she could smell my ground scent. Worried by the smaller buck, and beyond the point of caring about the doe's body language, the big buck charged forward. Both the doe and the smaller buck bounded out into the CRP grass on my side of the finger. The bigger buck, in turn,

This is the view that greeted the author when he followed up the blood trail and recovered his trophy. The buck's gross typical score is 185 inches.

stopped right where the doe had been–directly under my stand. That he smelled my scent can only be assumed, but that he was on my right side now–with me sitting–was a much more pressing emergency.

It seemed as if deer were crashing everywhere as I literally jumped to my feet and tried to draw my bow on the buck. For some reason, I couldn't get to full draw. I pulled back harder with my right elbow. No way! Suddenly my release arm shot forward and the arrow rattled against the bow. Surprisingly, the arrow didn't come off the string. The buck was still there, but with ears cupped my way, he was starting to walk warily out into the grass.

Fearing that something had gone wrong with my equipment, I quickly unclipped the release aid, removed the arrow, replaced it, rotated the peep sight, reattached the release and this time came easily to full draw. The buck was still within range, 25 yards out and angling way from me, walking parallel to the edge of the woods.

Remembering the low-light lesson I'd learned in October, I grunted loudly with my mouth to stop the buck for the shot. He took one more step and then froze–right behind the branches of a fallen tree. So much for stopping a walking buck! I looked for an opening but found none. Within seconds the buck was moving again. Briefly, I considered grunting a second time, but ditched the notion as I pulled my barely visible sight pins ahead of him.

Hurriedly, I guessed the range at 30 yards. When the correct pin settled on the buck's shoulder, I punched the release. "THUP." It sounded like I'd shot a watermelon. The buck's first reaction was to kick up his hind legs before busting through the finger of cover. Everything suggested a good vital hit, but as I replayed the shot in my mind, I began to suspect that the hit could have been several inches back of where I had planned. At worst, I figured I had struck liver–a very deadly hit, but one that you can't push.

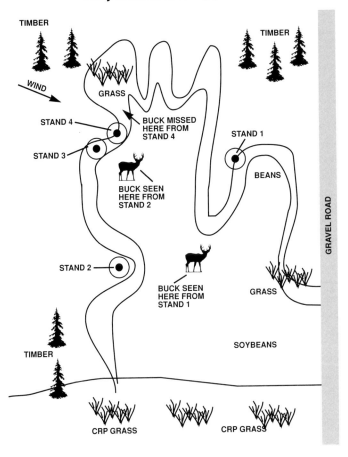

Early season feeding pattern

TIMBER

TIMBER

WIND

GRASS

STAND 4

BUCK MISSED
HERE FROM
STAND 4

STAND 1

STAND 3

BEANS

BUCK SEEN
HERE FROM
STAND 2

GRAVEL ROAD

STAND 2

BUCK SEEN
HERE FROM
STAND 1

GRASS

SOYBEANS

TIMBER

CRP GRASS

CRP GRASS

When trying to pattern a buck during the early season, it is critical that you hang back and observe from a safe distance until you have a good idea what is happening. You may only get one good hunt. It took several days before the author worked his way into position at Stand 4.

Travel routes during the rut

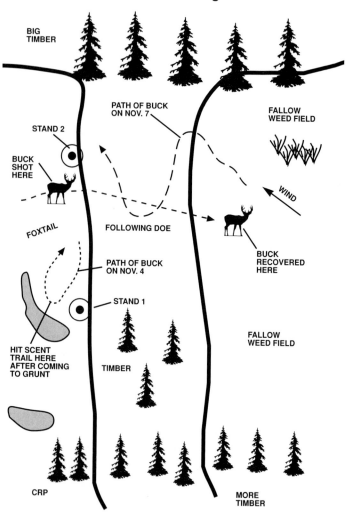

BIG TIMBER

PATH OF BUCK ON NOV. 7

FALLOW WEED FIELD

STAND 2

BUCK SHOT HERE

FOXTAIL

FOLLOWING DOE

WIND

PATH OF BUCK ON NOV. 4

BUCK RECOVERED HERE

STAND 1

HIT SCENT TRAIL HERE AFTER COMING TO GRUNT

FALLOW WEED FIELD

TIMBER

CRP

MORE TIMBER

The buck was first seen from Stand 1. It was here that he came almost all the way to the grunt call before smelling the author's scent in the tall foxtail grass. The buck was arrowed from Stand 2 three days later. He was following a doe through the bottleneck of this travel route.

I simply sat down in the tree and waited four hours. Surveying the situation more closely, I noticed the large limb that had prevented my elbow from fully extending on the straight down shot. A couple more nice bucks passed my tree as I relaxed and ate an early lunch. By the time I climbed down from the stand, I was confident he was dead somewhere close by.

The blood trail was light and washed out by the now melted frost. I easily followed the deep, running tracks as they angled 100 yards across the band of cover to the opposite edge. A large fallow field of shoulder-high weeds bordered the woods on that side, limiting visibility. I stood at the last blood and searched intently on the ground nearby. At one point, I thought I smelled a buck, but I dismissed the thought. Finally, I began glancing farther out, and was shocked to find that I was practically standing on him! Fifteen yards away I could see a heavy antler sticking above the short grass that grew under the overhanging limbs. There were six long points on it! I had killed the same giant buck that had come part way to my grunt call three days before!

STRATEGY SUMMARY

I adopted a low-impact strategy that kept me out of the big wooded areas on the farm. No doubt, these blocks of cover served as bedding areas and major rutting hubs. I had no intention of messing up such places. By staying out, I was able to keep the sensitive areas fresh while I waited along the fringe travel routes for something good to happen. It did, in a big way!

INDEX

Bold page numbers indicate photos or illustrations.

PHOTOGRAPHY CREDITS

Bill Winke: 7, 8, 11, 13, 21, 22, 25, 35, 36, 41, 49, 50, 56, 62, 66, 69, 77, 78, 83, 89, 91, 93, 101, 111, 112, 113, 117, 118, 120, 125, 129

Judd Cooney: 4, 74, 96

Steve Perlstein: 55

Charles J. Alsheimer: 18, 32, 108

Jeff Johnson: 60, 84, 99

Beth Winke: 43, 53, 65, 86

Mark Raycroft: 15, 94, onlay

Bill Marchel: 46, 71

Lon E. Lauber: 26, 70, 72

John Ford: 107